D0874059

GOD, MAN, AND SATAN

GOD, MAN, AND SATAN

Patterns of Christian Thought and Life in *Paradise Lost, Pilgrim's Progress,* and the Great Theologians

BY ROLAND MUSHAT FRYE

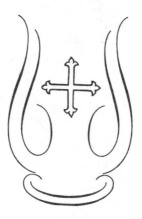

KENNIKAT PRESS
Port Washington, N. Y./London

TO

MY BONNIE JEAN

GOD, MAN, AND SATAN

Copyright © 1960 by Princeton University Press
Reissued in 1972 by Kennikat Press by arrangement
Library of Congress Catalog Card No: 70-159086
ISBN 0-8046-1628-0

Manufactured by Taylor Publishing Company   Dallas, Texas

ACKNOWLEDGMENTS

AT VARIOUS TIMES during the preparation of this book I was fortunate in obtaining assistance on particular problems from the following scholars: Gerald Eades Bentley of Princeton University; Louis B. Wright of the Folger Shakespeare Library; Paul Lehmann of Harvard University; Bard Thompson of Vanderbilt University; Hugh T. Kerr, Jr., and Émile Cailliet of Princeton Theological Seminary; John T. McNeill, Professor Emeritus of Union Theological Seminary; my graduate assistant, Miss Evelyn Harris, and my colleagues and students of Emory University. To Maurice Kelley of Princeton University, I owe lasting gratitude for my scholarly introduction to the exciting study of John Milton. No list, of course, can exhaust a writer's indebtedness, and no list can shift the responsibility for what he has written to shoulders other than his own, but it is always a pleasure to thank one's friends for the fruits of their friendship.

I am also indebted to the John Simon Guggenheim Foundation for the Fellowship which was granted to me for this work, and to Emory University for the year's leave of absence during which the work was completed. Emory University has, in addition, subsidized the publication of this study, as has the Princeton University Press by its allocation of funds granted from the Ford Foundation for supporting publication in the humanities and social sciences. For the generous support of these institutions I would express my thanks.

ACKNOWLEDGMENTS

And above all others there is my wife, who can never be thanked enough.

ROLAND MUSHAT FRYE

Emory University
February 2, 1960

CONTENTS

CONTENTS

[x]

INTRODUCTION

1

RELEVANT TRUTH

I. THE MATTER OF PERSPECTIVE

A PIOUS AGNOSTICISM is an essential part of the Christian faith. To know what God is in himself is beyond the powers of human thought, and is, indeed, irrelevant to human life. What may be known, and what man primarily needs to know, is what God is in relation to man and what man is in relation to God. Such needful and relevant knowledge is conveyed primarily not through the abstract propositions and definitions of philosophy, but through parables, actions, living symbols, and events. The poetic mode is thus particularly close to the heart of the Christian faith. Through the Biblical literature, the sacraments, and the symbols and theologies of the church, the Christian faith is taught.

It is also communicated through the great works of Christian imagination. Two of the greatest of these, John Milton's epic poem *Paradise Lost* and John Bunyan's prose allegory *Pilgrim's Progress*, are the focus of our study here. We shall approach them in the light of intelligible theological categories, setting up an interaction between the literary works and relevant theological understandings. By its very nature, such a process of interaction is not so much a matter of definitive statement as of discussion, exploration, and enlightenment. This process, moreover, should be especially helpful for

readers of *Paradise Lost* and *Pilgrim's Progress* who feel
the need for an interpretation of such subjects as heaven
and hell, angels and devils, in terms intelligible to the
modern mind.

Some half-century ago it was possible for a leading
literary scholar to refer to *Paradise Lost* as a monument
to dead ideas, and to do so not merely in reference to
his personal tastes but also to the current state of theology, which was certainly hibernating and apparently
dead. At that time the Christian ideas which *Paradise
Lost* treated had found no powerful modern idiom of
exposition in a vital, coherent, and intelligent theology.
Today the situation is radically changed, and whether
Christian ideas be accepted or rejected they are clearly
very much alive and part of the intellectual climate.
Thus although responsible critics may conclude that
the Christian ideas treated in *Paradise Lost* and *Pilgrim's Progress* are false ideas, no responsible criticism
today can refer to them as dead ideas. This change is in
large measure due, at least in Protestantism, to the
work of such distinguished contemporary thinkers as
Karl Barth, Reinhold Niebuhr, and John and Donald
Baillie, to name only a few.* This theological renewal

* Each of the theologians named above represents Reformed
or Neo-Reformation thought, and most of the theologians cited
in this work belong either to this tradition or to its Augustinian
and Pauline antecedents. Bunyan departed little from this tradition, and Milton's departures (for example, on the doctrines of
predestination and of the life everlasting) put him closer to
twentieth-century Neo-Reformation thought than to seventeenth-
century Protestant scholasticism. This tradition, indeed, seems
closest to representing a useful gloss on Milton and Bunyan, but
spokesmen for other traditions, too, are prominently represented
in my interpretation of the two works.

is not, of course, a totally new departure in Christianity, but bases itself in a recovery of major emphases in the Christian tradition going back to Augustine and beyond. Working in terms of the contemporary theological understanding, therefore, we will cite fathers of the church, medieval scholastics, and reformers, as well as living writers, in approaching our subject.

Milton and Bunyan have as much to contribute to contemporary Christian thought as contemporary Christian thought has to provide, in the way of an introduction, to understanding Milton and Bunyan. I shall attempt in this study to interrelate the insights of the renascence of Christian thought with *Paradise Lost* and *Pilgrim's Progress*. The result will not be a scholarly reconstruction of the seventeenth-century *weltanschauungen* of Milton and Bunyan, an important area of inquiry which has been effectively treated by many able scholars. It may, nevertheless, better prepare us to appreciate the intentions of both men than would an archaeological exegesis, however accurate or significant. Similarly, the literary symbols, although they are not to be unilaterally equated with any theological definitions, may enliven and deepen the theological vision.

We are dealing here with two literary masterpieces which are very much alive, and with a religious tradition also very much alive. The two areas can be related "definitively" only if we treat both as closed, finished, and fossilized, arresting and objectifying the literary works and the religious understanding to correlate them precisely. This would be possible if we were, for instance, to examine Milton and Bunyan in terms of their own specifically seventeenth-century Puritan theologies. Great advantages are inherent in such an objectified approach, which applies something of the accuracy of laboratory dissection to literary studies, but this is not our approach here. What we seek to establish here is a vital interaction between living literature and living thought, rather than a final statement of either. By this interplay we may be prepared to turn to the documents with a broadened understanding of their issues, and with the intellectual enthusiasm necessary for a continuing and significant concern with them and with their major problem: human existence.

Both Milton and Bunyan were essentially didactic in intent, their concern being the effective treatment of Christian faith and life. John Milton states his purpose in the prayer with which *Paradise Lost* opens:

> What in me is dark
> Illumine, what is low raise and support;
> That to the height of this great argument
> I may assert eternal providence,
> And justify the ways of God to men.† (I, 22-26)

Milton's large concern, then, is with an understanding of the Christian faith. For Bunyan, the focus is on implementing the Christian life. In the verses introducing his prose allegory, Bunyan declares his intention:

> This book will make a traveller of thee,
> If by its counsel thou wilt ruled be;

† Quotations from *Paradise Lost* are identified by parenthetical references to book and line numbers.

It will direct thee to the Holy Land,
If thou wilt its directions understand.‡ (7)

This is not to say, of course, that Milton is unconcerned with the working Christian life, or that Bunyan
is indifferent to the structure of the faith. Both men are
patently concerned, as we shall see, with both aspects
of Christianity, but their primary focusing is different.
We shall therefore consider *Paradise Lost* primarily in
connection with the Christian vision of reality, and
Pilgrim's Progress primarily in connection with the dis-
tinctive life of the Christian. To achieve a more meaningful introduction to the literary works, and to indicate
something of the richness and depth of the ideas conveyed through them, we shall deal both with the patterns of literature and the patterns of Christian thought.
By drawing on the skills of literature and of theology
we will exhaust and define the meaning of neither, but
we may find what is, in some measure at least, a fresh
and enlightening approach to *Paradise Lost*, to *Pilgrim's
Progress*, and to the Christian understanding of man's
life under God.

II. THE METHOD OF ACCOMMODATION

"I am persuaded," Martin Luther wrote, "that without skill in literature genuine theology cannot stand,
just as hitherto in the ruin and prostration of letters
it too has miserably fallen and been laid low." Indeed,
Luther felt that the Reformation's rediscovery of "the

‡ Quotations from *Pilgrim's Progress* are identified by parenthetical references to page numbers in the standard Wharey edition, published at Oxford by the Clarendon Press in 1928.

remarkable disclosure of the Word of God would not have taken place had God not first prepared the way by the rediscovery of language and sciences, as by Baptist fore-runners."[1] There is one very real sense in which the Reformation was a scholar's movement: the application of the literary skills of Renaissance intellectuals to the Biblical literature.[2] The very core of the literary mode is central here. There is the nurture of the imagination, and the development of a power to analyze thought which goes beyond the surface, which sees through the symbol to its larger referent, but which remains faithful to the symbol itself. To the great Reformers, the exposition of Scripture was a *literary* analysis, and when they emphasized the level of the *litera* they were not calling for mechanical concentration on what the modern fundamentalist means by literalism, any more than was Thomas Aquinas when he placed the same emphasis on the literal level "from which alone we can argue."[3] They were, rather, calling for a concern with the literary meaning of the text considered by the best methods available to the Christian humanist. They would rescue Scripture from the fantastic embellish-

[1] Martin Luther, "Letter to Eoban Hess, March 29, 1523," in *Werke*, Weimar Edition, *Briefwechsel*, Vol. III, 50. Quoted by John T. McNeill, "History of the Interpretation of the Bible: Mediaeval and Reformation Period," *The Interpreter's Bible*, 12 vols., ed. Nolan B. Harmon (New York: Abingdon-Cokesbury, 1952-57), Vol. I, p. 123.

[2] E. Harris Harbison, *The Christian Scholar in the Age of Reformation* (New York: Charles Scribner's Sons, 1956), *passim*.

[3] Thomas Aquinas, *The Summa Theologica*, I, Q. 1, Art. 10, trans. A. M. Fairweather, in *Nature and Grace* (Philadelphia: Westminster Press, 1954).

ments of scholastic ingenuity. They would do so not only in terms of the "proper" meaning of simple statements, but also by organic reference to metaphoric and to compound or composite meanings,[4] in terms of a fully literary exegesis, in order to discover the full meaning of the text itself. Thus, according to Luther, "without skill in literature genuine theology cannot stand."[5]

Of primary importance here is the doctrine of accommodation, by which God's reality is typologically reduced from incomprehensibility and expressed in terms "accommodated" to human understanding. The use of accommodation was not a Reformation invention, of course; we find Thomas Aquinas writing that "poetry uses metaphors to depict, since men naturally find pictures pleasing. But sacred doctrine uses them because they are necessary and useful."[6] Although the reformers did not invent the doctrine of accommodation, they used it repeatedly. John Calvin's interpretation is illustrative for our immediate purposes, especially in view of his influence on the Puritan movement, to which both Milton and Bunyan belonged. Fully aware of the broader elements of literary method and of its relevance to the Biblical tradition, Calvin taught that Scripture does not plainly express what God is, but adapts the understanding of him to human capacity, for while we are in an earthly condition "we need symbols or mirrors to exhibit to us the appearance of spiritual and heavenly

[4] Heinrich Heppe, *Reformed Dogmatics, Set Out And Illustrated From The Sources* (London: George Allen and Unwin, 1950), pp. 37-39.
[5] "Letter to Eoban Hess, March 29, 1523," *op.cit.*, p. 123.
[6] *Summa Theologica*, I, Q. 1, Art. 9.

things in a kind of earthly way."[7] These symbols do not show us "what God is in himself, but what he is to us"[8] (*non quis sit apud se, sed qualis erga nos*) and so "there is no need for the reality to agree at all points with the symbol, if only it suit sufficiently for the purpose of symbolizing."[9]

This is a point of utmost importance: a one-to-one equation between the Christian symbol and its referent is not to be expected. In the third chapter of Matthew, for example, there is the statement that after the baptism of Jesus the Spirit of God descended upon him in the likeness of a dove. In commenting on this account, Calvin remarks that although John the Baptist "says that he saw the Holy Spirit descending," he actually saw only a dove, and not the Holy Spirit at all. Nonetheless, Calvin adds, the vision was not "an empty figure" but an efficient "sign" of the presence of the Holy Spirit in Christ, represented to John according to his capacity.[10] Similarly, Calvin denies that the risen Christ is actually seated on the right hand of the Father, but even while denying the literal accuracy of such descriptions he accepts their metaphorical truth.[11] Thus in connection with the final judgment, Calvin treats the apocalyptic symbols in terms of their ultimate meaning, that God will totally conquer all sin and evil, rather

[7] John Calvin, *Theological Treatises*, trans. and ed. J. K. S. Reid (Philadelphia: Westminster Press, 1954), p. 131.
[8] John Calvin, *The Institutes of the Christian Religion*, trans. John Allen (Philadelphia: Presbyterian Board of Publications), n.d., I, X, 2.
[9] *Theological Treatises*, p. 112.
[10] *Ibid.*, p. 147.
[11] *Ibid.*, p. 101.

than of their literal content. He therefore interprets the last trumpet as metaphorical, and writes that "the fact that the stars fall from heaven is not to be understood literally, but as an image adapted to our capacities of understanding."[12]

These and other images represent the accommodation of God's truth to man's capacities. Calvin repeatedly insists that at every point of revelation the principle of accommodation always intervenes between God and man.[13] In this, he and the leading Reformers generally are supported by the great mainstream of Christian interpretation: God's truth is accommodated to human understanding through events and symbols, and primarily through the Incarnation. In the patristic period, Athanasius wrote of the divine revelation that as a "teacher who cares for his disciples, if some of them cannot profit by higher subjects, comes down to their level, and teaches them at any rate by simpler courses, so also did the Word of God."[14] Similarly, what Calvin called accommodation and understood in terms of metaphors, symbols, and figures of speech, the twentieth-century Biblical theologian John Knox refers to as transfiguration, defined as "falsification at one level for the sake of truth at another, infidelity to fact for the sake

[12] Heinrich Quistorp, *Calvin's Doctrine of the Last Things*, trans. Harold Knight (Richmond: John Knox Press, 1955), pp. 123-24, 142.

[13] Edward A. Dowey, Jr., *The Knowledge of God in Calvin's Theology* (New York: Columbia University Press, 1952), p. 10.

[14] Edward R. Hardy and Cyril C. Richardson, eds., *Christology of the Later Fathers* (Philadelphia: Westminster Press, 1954), p. 69.

of fidelity to meaning."[15] The same conception is found in Thomas Aquinas when he writes, of "parabolical meaning," that "when Scripture speaks of the arm of the Lord, the literal sense is not that God has such a bodily member, but that he has what such a bodily member indicates, namely active power."[16]

Calvin repeatedly emphasizes the accommodated nature of such anthropomorphism,[17] which he describes as being really a form of baby talk, wherein God reveals himself by speaking "as it were childishly, as nurses do." Such images and expressions "do not so plainly express what God is, as they do apply the understanding of him to our slender capacity."[18] This is not to say, however, that we are to dismiss such figures of speech as "mere" symbols, and settle on an abstract conception of God as a more accurate description than any other. Although symbols are not identical with what they symbolize, and are not to be clung to in their visible signs, they do communicate in a definite way by the direction of their meaning. Symbols for deity do not just refer to the word "god" or "gods," but carry, if they have any communicative value, definite notions as to what the word "god" refers to. To say that the great religions refer in one way or another through symbols to "god" or "gods" may be true enough, but it is not a very significant observation. What is important is the

[15] John Knox, *On the Meaning of Christ* (New York: Charles Scribner's Sons, 1947), p. 80.

[16] *Theologica*, I, Q. 1, Art. 10.

[17] Dowey, *op.cit.*, pp. 243-44.

[18] John Calvin, *The Institutes of Christian Religion*, trans. Thomas Norton (London: John Norton, 1611), I, xiii, 1.

conception of deity conveyed by the symbols used. Symbols communicate meaning, and different symbolic systems communicate different meanings.

Our concern is with the Christian system of symbols, which is based largely on the analogy of personality. God, though in his essence beyond human comprehension, is to be dealt with as a person, rather than as an abstraction or an absolute. The personal quality of God is conveyed through virtually every revealing accommodation of the Biblical symbols, as, for example, in the anthropomorphic "baby talk," and is ultimately manifested in the historical person of the incarnate Son in a way which is unique, final, adequate, and indispensable. Throughout the Christian Scriptures and the Christian tradition, we are repeatedly faced with the teaching, through symbols and through history, that God cannot be dealt with as an abstraction, but only as a person, and as the personal God and Father of Jesus Christ. This is the ultimate terminus of the Christian symbols.

III. THE METHOD OF INTERPRETATION

John Milton and John Bunyan fully understood the important place of accommodation in the Christian faith. Milton acknowledged the accommodated nature of Scriptural teaching in this way: "Our safest way is to form in our minds such a conception of God, as shall correspond with his own delineation and representation of himself in the sacred writings. For granted that both in the literal and figurative descriptions of God, he is exhibited not as he really is, but in such a manner as may be within the scope of our comprehensions, yet we ought to maintain such a conception of him as he, in condescending to accommodate himself to our capacities, has shown that he desires we should conceive. For it is on this very account that he has lowered himself to our level, lest in our flights above the reach of human understanding, and beyond the written word of Scripture, we should be tempted to indulge in vague cogitations and subtleties."[19]

Milton makes clear that the method of accommodation as operative in Scripture is also the basic mode of development in *Paradise Lost*, as the angelic Raphael tells Adam:

> . . . what surmounts the reach
> Of human sense, I shall delineate so,
> By lik'ning spiritual to corporal forms,
> As may express them best, though what if Earth
> Be but the shadow of heav'n, and things therein
> Each to other like, more than on earth
>   is thought? (v. 571-76)

The same point is made repeatedly in *Paradise Lost*, as Milton reiterates his understanding of the fact that "both in the literal and figurative descriptions," divine truth is exhibited not as it really is, but as men can best comprehend it.

Thus the scientific accuracy of the accounts of the

[19] John Milton, "De Doctrina Christiana," trans. Charles Sumner, *The Works of John Milton*, ed. Frank A. Patterson, et al. (New York: Columbia University Press, 1933), Vol. XIV, pp. 31, 33.

creation and fall is irrelevant. When the question arose as to certain astronomical inaccuracies, indeed impossibilities, in the first chapter of Genesis, Calvin remarked of the author of the account that "as was proper to a theologian, he had regard to men rather than stars," and was interested in instructing man in his human nature and destiny rather than in astronomy.[20] The central conception here is of an existential truth, a truth relevant to man's present condition and his ultimate redemption. The truth of the Genesis accounts is a figurative truth; that is, it is both figurative and true. The key to this conception, which will dominate our treatment both of *Paradise Lost* and *Pilgrim's Progress*, may be found in the words of the sixteenth-century Reformer, Amandus Polanus. The true or genuine, he said, "is not opposed to the figurative but to the false."[21]

It is in precisely the same terms that Bunyan would have us understand his allegory. Criticized for having written in the metaphoric mode, Bunyan replied that he was merely following the example of Scripture:

> . . . was not God's laws,
> His Gospel-laws in olden times held forth
> By types, shadows and metaphors?
>
> . . . .
>
> The prophets used much by metaphors
> To set forth truth; yea, who so considers
> Christ, his apostles too, shall plainly see
> That truths, to this day, in such mantles be.
>   (4 and 5)

[20] Dowey, *op.cit.*, p. 141.
[21] Heppe, *op.cit.*, p. 638.

Bunyan repeatedly emphasizes these points in the verses with which he prefaces his allegory and through which he presents his literary intention and theory. So, again on the symbolic method, he writes:

> I find that Holy Writ in many places,
> Hath semblance with this method,
>   where the cases
> Do call for one thing to set forth another. (6)

He uses the method, then, because he regards it as the most effective way to communicate the truths with which he deals:

> Use it I may then, and yet nothing smother
> Truth's golden beams; Nay, by this method may
> Make it cast forth its rays as light as day. (6)

In this fashion, he says,

> I also know, a dark similitude
> Will on the fancy more itself intrude,
> And will stick faster in the heart and head,
> Than things from similies not borrowed. (181)

He then advises his readers to "turn up my metaphors" (174), and determine their deeper significance rather than concentrate childishly on their literal significance. One more dose of Bunyan's doggerel verse will be needed to complete his case:

> Take heed also that thou be not extreme
> In playing with the *outside* of my dream;
> Nor let my figure or similitude
> Put thee into a laughter or a feud.

Leave this for *boys* and *fools*: but as for thee,
Do thou the substance of my matter see. (174)

The substance of the matter is precisely what we shall attempt to understand as we "turn up" the metaphors through which the Christian life and faith are treated in *Paradise Lost* and *Pilgrim's Progress*. To this end we shall draw freely on the great theologians, both those who lived before and those who have lived since the time of Milton and Bunyan. Even though many of these men could not possibly have read what our seventeenth-century authors wrote, or have influenced them in the writing of it, they certainly knew what Milton and Bunyan were talking about, and can help the modern reader to understand it, too. Thus in trying to discern the meaning of the demonic, we shall draw on the writings of men as remote from each other in time, place, and specific theological orientation, as John Chrysostom and Karl Barth, Augustine of Hippo and Denis de Rougemont. In the explication of symbols we shall, indeed, draw on every source in the Christian tradition that appears both useful and applicable; but throughout, the primary purpose will be to develop an understanding meaningful to twentieth-century man.

PART ONE

Paradise Lost and the
Christian Vision

2

SATAN: THE CHARACTER
OF EVIL

I. THE DEMONIC SYMBOLS

MEN WHO ARE THOUGHTFUL as well as sensitive to the
tragedies of human existence, so long as they continue
both to think and to feel, cannot ignore the problem
of evil. An inescapable aspect of all human life, it has
been dealt with by differing strategies within different
traditions. One of these strategies denies the basic reality of evil, reduces it to the status of illusion, mirage,
maya, giving it only a deceptive appearance of reality
within a great all-encompassing monism, while another
treats evil as one ultimate aspect of a dual reality, gives
it an actual place within a total though divided scheme
of existence, and sets it off as an antagonist of good in
an equal division of forces within the universe.

In its own doctrine of evil, Christianity accepts neither
view, but uses symbols like those found in both these
treatments. The reality of evil is not denied, yet it is
regarded as only a perversion of real existence. Its attractive power is admitted, yet held to be a strictly in-
ferior power. Thus the Christian maintains neither the
monist nor the dualist solution of the problem of evil,
but accepts the reality of evil while holding that it is
both subordinate and perverse.

[21]

Christianity summarizes the source of evil under the symbol of the demonic, and the essence of the demonic is the aspiration to godhead, the attempt to usurp the place of the Creator, followed by assault upon creation in a frenzy of hate which irrevocably dedicates itself to a continuous destruction of life. Satan is thus *the* continuous source of evil. As Antichrist, Calvin called him "the sphere of atrocity and horror under the name of a person."[1] He is not an independent evil being set opposite an equally independent good being, and his fall from heaven comes precisely from his false claim to be just that. Essentially irrational, teleologically undefinable, Satan is, as Denis de Rougemont says, the "absolute anti-model."[2] St. John Chrysostom has it that he is mania, frenzy, impossible to reduce to rationality,[3] while Emil Brunner says that the demonic defies all precise definition.[4] With Satan, as elsewhere, we are brought back to "accommodation," to the symbolic and metaphoric treatment of a force which may be fully interpreted in no other terms.

In the Christian conception, then, evil is totally subordinate to God: it is good in its created intention, but perverted from its normative goals. In poetic terms, Satan is a perversion of the great, but subordinate, good, which was Lucifer. As Paul Tillich says, "the demonic

[1] Quistorp, *op.cit.*, p. 119.
[2] Denis de Rougemont, *The Devil's Share*, trans. Haakon Chevalier (New York: Bollingen Series II, 1952), p. 14.
[3] Bernard Leeming, "The Adversary," *Satan* (New York: Sheed and Ward, 1952), p. 39.
[4] Emil Brunner, *Dogmatics: The Christian Doctrine of Creation and Redemption*, trans. Olive Wyon (London: Lutterworth Press, 1955), Vol. II, pp. 142-143.

is the elevation of something conditional to unconditional significance."[5] It is thus basically a lie, carrying at the core of its existence a falsification of its own nature. As evil itself, it cannot be denied, but must not be made absolute. In its relation to man, its power should not be underestimated, yet in relation to God it is as nothing. It can be intelligently treated, Barth says, only through fantasy and poetry.[6] It is in precisely these terms that Milton does treat it, as he develops a portrait of evil unsurpassed for the profundity of its insight, and for the breadth and balance of its vision.

The thrust of Satan's aspiration is to enjoy himself rather than God, to become the bearer of his own image, to become power without love. Augustine wrote that "the bad angel loved himself more than God, refused to be subject to God, swelled with pride, came short of supreme being, and fell." It was a totally free choice, as all declare, including Satan himself—a choice left to his own will. The righteousness of God's judgment consists, as Karl Barth puts it, in the fact that he gives the creature what it chooses for itself.[7] Lucifer's choice was himself, not God. Thus, Augustine says again, "he became less than he had been, because, in wishing to enjoy his own power rather than God's, he wished to enjoy

[5] Paul Tillich, *Systematic Theology* (Chicago: The University of Chicago Press, 1951), Vol. I, p. 140.

[6] Otto Weber, *Karl Barth's Church Dogmatics, An Introductory Report on Volume I:1 to III:4*, trans. Arthur C. Cochrane (Philadelphia: Westminster Press, 1953), p. 196, hereafter referred to as *Barth's Dogmatics*.

[7] Karl Barth, *Dogmatics in Outline*, trans. G. T. Thompson (New York: Philosophical Library, 1950), p. 118, hereafter referred to as *Outline*.

what was less."[8] He made it his chief end to glorify and enjoy himself forever, in short, to be God. Hell for him is existence as his own deity. "To set himself in glory above his peers," as Milton writes in *Paradise Lost*, "He trusted to have equalled the most High" (I, 39-40).

Having briefly noticed the role assigned to Satan by Christian theology, let us turn to the structure of *Paradise Lost* before developing in more detail Satan's place within it. The epic opens in hell. The first two books are devoted to the fiery lake in which the rebellious legions find themselves, and to their building there of a kingdom of evil. A great demonic council is held, in which a plan of destruction is settled upon, and Satan himself volunteers for the role of counterfeit messiah dedicated to the betrayal of man. In the third book, the scene is shifted to heaven, where the plan of salvation is projected as the Son willingly casts himself in the role of man's suffering redeemer. Later in this book, Satan, like a vulture, is seen approaching the world; book four is devoted to Satan's first prospectus of earth and of man's life upon it, as well as to his first unsuccessful tempting of Eve in her dream. He is discovered crouching by her ear in the form of a toad, and is dismissed by the angelic guard. The four following books are devoted to the angelic Raphael's visit to Adam. In books five and six, Raphael warns Adam of Satan's intentions, and tells him of the war in heaven and of the expulsion of the rebellious angels. In the seventh book, Raphael recounts the course of creation, and in the fol-

[8] *Earlier Writings*, trans. and ed. John H. S. Burleigh (Philadelphia: Westminster Press, 1953), p. 237.

lowing, Adam tells his own story as he recalls it. The ninth book is given to the fall of man under the demonic temptation, and to the resulting changes in Adam and Eve. In the tenth book, the Son pronounces sentence upon man, at the same time sentencing himself to the cross, and Satan commissions his two offspring, Sin and Death, for the ravin of earth. Adam and Eve are moved to prayer, and the two final books of the epic are devoted to their reconciliation and to Adam's vision of the course of human history, under the tutelage of the angelic Michael.

Man's place within this total picture, and the relation of God to him, will be treated in later chapters, but let us now examine closely the figure to whom Milton first introduces us—Satan. We must remember throughout that the purpose of the Satanic symbol, as developed in Christianity and as projected by Milton, is an interpretation of a certain type of life, a type which is always present as an open alternative for man, and of the relation which it produces between Creator and creature on one level, and between creature and creature on another. The treatment of Satan is important, therefore, not as a metaphysical construction, not as an instance of curious and fascinating speculation, but as a commentary on life, on human frustration and fulfillment. This point should be kept in mind at every stage of the development. The demonic symbolism provides not a "mere" mythology, however beautiful or frightful or impressive or accurate, but a strategy for understanding, and so for dealing with, certain inescapable aspects of the reality living men must face. Throughout, the treatment is figurative, but this does not mean that it is ungenuine. The genuine, as Polanus said, "is not opposed to the figurative but to the false."[9]

II. THE PRETENSE OF DEITY

Whereas God's being is an organic symmetry of love and power, a symmetry clearly revealed in the Son, Satan's concern in usurping the godhead is only for power. His "Imperial Sov'ranty" in hell is "adorn'd With splendor, arm'd with power" (II, 446-47), but devoid of love. "What can Heav'n show more" than magnificence, asks Mammon (II, 273), thereby displaying the demonic concentration. Magnificence is the panoply of power, and, to the demonic, heaven appears to be no more. Satan's revolt is not only that of the subordinate part against the source of wholeness, but also the attempt to usurp control of all things by regarding godhead as a fragment of itself, as mere naked power, divorced from love and from goodness. Indeed, within this fragmental conception of deity, Satan achieves his end, for he is worshipped by his retinue, "high in the midst exalted as a God" (VI, 99 and II, 479); nonetheless he reigns only as the "*Idol* of majesty divine" (VI, 101) because he is a parody of the true God he wishes to replace. Having repudiated his own just possibilities, which could have been realized, Satan by his usurpation makes any fulfillment impossible. Even the lower creature, man, can attain fulfillment, while Satan "still unfulfill'd with pain of longing pines" (IV, 511).

[9] Heppe, *op.cit.*, p. 638.

The choice is free and deliberate, and once made is never repudiated. "Better to reign in hell than serve in heav'n" (i, 263), Satan says, for he has sealed himself. The more he strives after the power of God, the more he accomplishes his own unfulfillment; the more strenuously he attempts to "reascend, Self-raised" (i, 633-34), the more he achieves his own self-damnation. Here we have the central irony of his rhetorical "awake, arise, or be forever fall'n" (i, 330), spoken from the fiery lake of hell.

It was Satan's "confidence to equal God in power" (vi, 343), but by this assertion of autonomy he gains only the knowledge that God is indeed almighty (i, 143-45), a gain which can scarcely be regarded as constructive information under the circumstances, and which should be recalled in connection with his unqualified (and hypocritical) praise of knowledge to Eve. Since all power is God's, Satan's active power is limited to perversion, to the fragmentary pushing of order over into anarchy. Thus he leagues himself with Chaos: "yours be th' advantage all, mine the revenge" (ii, 987). As Barth puts it, "this intoxicating thought of power is chaos."[10] So, on his journey towards the seduction of man, Satan courts Chaos, Milton's brilliant personification of anarchy and disorder, with the promise that he will "reduce" the created cosmos "to her original darkness and your sway" (ii, 983-84). His power cannot enable him ever to destroy creation, but his perversions of it are precisely in the direction of atomism and

[10] *Outline*, p. 48.

[27]

anarchy, the reduction of harmony, the extension of discord and decay.

Satan's antagonism to the created order, though clear throughout Milton's epic, is first exhibited in his demagogic repudiation of the fact of creation, as he harangues his rebellious legions in heaven with the pretension that he and they owe their existence only to themselves, "self-begot, self-rais'd By our own quick'ning power" so that "our puissance is our own" (v, 860-64). The very fact of creation is denied, for that fact is the basis for dependence, whereas autogeny is the basis for autonomy. Satan has become the first Manichee, the first propagandist for the equal and independent existence of rival deities, good and evil.

This denial of creation in order to assert autonomy is, as Satan knows and admits to himself, a lie (IV, 42-45). The repudiation of the sovereignty of God and the reality of creation is, in effect, the repudiation of an objective basis for truth; when Satan declares the doctrine of his own self-creation and his own deity, he thereby declares himself the final authority over truth. Standing now as the antagonist of Creator and of creation, he operates through the perversion of truth and the invention of lies. As the prime "artificer of fraud" (IV, 121), he repeatedly denies the objective order by fabricating falsehood. His pretense of autogeny is one example, his treacherous appeal for "peace and composure" (VI, 560) during the war in heaven is another, while the entire temptation of Eve is a fabric woven of half truths and whole falsehoods, as the master of counterfeit works out his attack upon the harmony of creation.

The lie, however, is only one of the devices by which Satan denies the created order. His repudiation of creation in general is expressed through a manifold and expanding hate. On earth, he first declares his hatred of the sun's light (IV, 37), and proceeds to demonstrate his hatred of all life, a general indifference to all that lives, as he sits upon the Tree of Life in the guise of a cormorant "devising death" (IV, 197). To him, the life in Eden is only a background against which he can plot the destruction of men, a "fair foundation laid whereon to build Their ruin" (IV, 521-22). So, too, the created joys of married love inspire in him only a "jealous leer malign" and the urge to disrupt (IV, 503), to substitute woe for joy, long woes for pleasure (IV, 368-69, 535). The garden, expressing the goal of creation in harmonious order, beauty and communion, elicits from Satan only the response of destructive envy, as he "saw undelighted all delight" (IV, 286).

The repudiation of creation is inseparable from Satan's willed incapacity for submitting as a part to the harmonious enjoyment of the whole under God. "Participation" is now impossible for Satan *as* Satan, although it had been the core of his existence in heaven as Lucifer, and he substitutes for it a drive for domination, a rabid possessiveness which asserts itself by control over others. Self-acceptance is possible for the demonic only by means of the incorporation of other selves, as though the self could only buttress its selfhood by reducing other selves to serfdom or by destroying

[29]

them. The central purpose of Satanic life is "to waste [God's] creation or possess" (II, 365), and it becomes increasingly clear that the rule which Satan seeks is possible only through the ruin of other creatures. That is the ultimate meaning of demonic possession.

It is basic to Milton's epic, and to Christianity in general, that the created order is good. Against this good in all its forms, as well as against the divine source of all goodness, Satan reacts, when he declares the creed of hell: "Evil be thou my good" (IV, 110). "Evil," says Albert Schweitzer "is what annihilates, hampers or hinders life."[11] Satan chooses this as his mode of existence.

But Satan cannot attack creation without damaging himself. Even if his attempts at the perversion of other creatures were to be defeated, he could pervert himself, could degrade that creature which is Satan and was Lucifer, for had all others repudiated his repudiation of their own creation, the very fact of his frenzy of destruction would have denigrated himself. Inescapably connected with his statement that "only in destroying I find ease," comes his admission that "thereby worse to me redounds" (IX, 128-29). The point is repeated for emphasis, and it is continually given dramatic representation in the actual degeneration of Satan. His self-assertion amounts to self-rejection in the central irony of the choice by which, in seeking to exalt himself above the scale of life, he actually precipitates himself, beneath all creation and all life, into the abyss of hell.

[11] Albert Schweitzer, "The Ethics of Reverence for Life," *Christendom*, Vol. I (Winter, 1936), p. 230.

III. THE LIFE OF ANTICHRIST

The primary target of Satan's animus and envy is the Son. These two, the Son and Satan, are precisely and dramatically opposite, and here we see another instance of Satan's distortion of deity, in the impossible concentration on power apart from love. The revolt in heaven originated in his "grieving to see [the Son's] glory" (VI, 792). In his envious and self-induced blindness to the fact that in the Son "love hath abounded more than glory abounds" (III, 312), Satan harangues his troops that the Son "hath to himself ingross't All power" (V, 775-76), while in his own power-madness he ignores the far more important fact that in the Son "the fulness dwells of love divine" (III, 225). The Son sets aside his infinite power in order to express his love, whereas Satan exiles love (and with it, himself) in order to express his limited power. Insisting that he was "ordain'd to govern, not to serve" (V, 802), Satan willingly "quits all" to dominate and destroy, whereas the Son, though "equal to God, and equally enjoying Godlike fruition," himself willingly "quitted all" in order to serve and preserve (III, 306-7).

The conflict of Christ and Antichrist is explicitly and repeatedly underscored in *Paradise Lost*, so that it becomes a major theme of the epic. In passing judgment on man after the fall, the Son is seen to be in fact most full of "favor, grace, and mercy" even when "angry most he seem'd and most severe" (X, 1095-96), whereas Satan as the serpent tempting man to fall is in fact most severe and hateful even when he seems most solicitous

[31]

and concerned for human good. Satan throughout op-
poses envy, despair, and hate to faith, hope, and charity,
strife to peace, misery to joy, pain to blessedness and
felicity. To the divine will that "earth be chang'd to
heav'n, and heav'n to earth, One kingdom, joy and
union without end" (VII, 160-61), Satan counterposes
his own plan for "earth and hell To mingle and in-
volve" (II, 383-84), to make of hell and earth "one
realm, one continent Of easy thoroughfare" (X, 392-93).
The two purposes differ as the monarchical pride of
Satan differs from the "fulness . . . of love divine" in
the Son (III, 225). The extension of heaven is the extension of life, that of hell the extension of death, and
as against the joys of heaven the "joys" of hell are the
perverted delights of sadism, finding ease only in insatiable destruction.

In opposition to the divine love, Satan dedicates himself to "immortal hate" (I, 107), establishing at the core
of his existence the hatred of God and of man. Seeing
Eve, he declares that though she is fit for the love of
gods, there is for him a terror in love when it is

> . . . not approacht by stronger hate,
> Hate stronger, under show of love well-feign'd,
> The way which to her ruin now I tend.
>   (IX, 490-93)

His constant armor is hate, and his design the spread
of enmity between man and man, and God and man.
His own hatred is all-inclusive: he curses the love of
God and then proceeds to curse himself (IV, 69-71), for
his hatred of others is inextricably involved with the

hatred of himself. Immediately, as if to identify hell with the hatred of God and of self, comes the awesome demonic cry, "which way I fly is hell; myself am hell" (IV, 75).

Satan's assertion that he was "ordain'd to govern, not to serve" (v, 802) is at one with his repudiation of love. In direct contrast to the fallen angel, Satan, stands the faithful Raphael, who, in telling Adam of the heavenly hosts, declares that "freely we serve Because we freely love" (v, 538-39), service being the free expression of love. Again, Satan's repudiation of service, of subordination, of creation, is a part of his repudiation of love. In place of love there is only "fierce desire" (IV, 509), an incorporative, omnivorous possessiveness which would feed all life into itself. Against this linked hatred and desire moves the love of God in the primary dimension of the conflict, so that the final victory of Christ over Antichrist will come only when "heav'nly love shall outdo hellish hate" (III, 298).

But although the conflict may be seen primarily in terms of love and hate, it has other almost equally important dimensions. One of these is the conflict of reason with unreason, closely related to the demonic lust for power and apotheosis of force, as seen in Abdiel's challenge to Satan that it is brutish "when reason hath to deal with force" (VI, 125). Satan's reliance on power represents an exclusion of reason as well as of love, or, perhaps more accurately, one cannot be excluded without the other. "The principle of reason which governs the world," according to Archbishop William Temple, "is the eternal victory of love over selfishness,"[12] and it is precisely this "principle of reason" which Satan denies by the victory within himself of "selfishness" over love. But the matter goes further. Reason is judgment which accords with the scale of values incorporated by the Creator in creation, and Satan has repudiated all—values, Creator and creation. His judgment accords only with his own pride and self-deceit, as we have already observed in his falsifying view of God, man, and nature. Thus God the Father describes the demonic revolt as a revolt from reason: the fallen angels

> . . . reason for their law refuse,
> Right reason for their law, and for their King
> Messiah, who by right of merit reigns. (VI, 41-43)

Reason, in Milton, is repeatedly linked with freedom. True liberty, Michael tells Adam, "with right reason dwells Twinn'd, and from her hath no dividual being" (XII, 84-85). Love, reason, freedom: the three are indissolubly connected, and Satan fell from all three. "Freely we serve, Because we freely love," says Raphael, "in this we stand or fall, and some are fall'n" (V, 538-41). Satan and God agree in this, if in nothing else, that "freely they stood who stood, and fell who fell" (III, 102).

Satan's fall from freedom was the arbitrary denial of his own potential, the arbitrary substitution of a potential impossible to realize; he thus feels an immortal frustration and the ever-present "torment within me,

---

[12] William Temple, *Foundations: A Statement of Christian Belief in Terms of Modern Thought, by Seven Oxford Men* (London: Macmillan and Company, 1912), pp. 221-22.

as from the hateful siege Of contraries" (IX, 121-22). As a result of his choice, he becomes a slave to what would, psychologically, be called an "ego-ideal," a substitute or ersatz self, an identification of the self with an impossible image. It is because of this slavery of Satan to a self-created idol of himself that Abdiel accuses him of being "to thyself enthrall'd" (VI, 181).

On the understanding of freedom, classical Reformation theology and modern psychoanalysis are in general agreement, as the following quotations from the sixteenth-century theologian Ursinus and the contemporary psychologist Patrick Mullahy will suggest. According to Ursinus, freedom is the individual's capacity to act on its own judgment "in accordance with the order congruent with its nature, and to enjoy the good things suited to it, without prohibition or hindrance, and not to sustain defects or burdens not proper to its nature."[13] Mullahy writes in a strikingly similar vein that "to be free is to be able to act in accordance with the powers that one possesses under the conditions of human life. . . . In other words, man is free when he is determined by the requirements and conditions of his own nature; and only when he expresses his nature can values and ideals have genuine authority and appeal."[14]

Satan's repudiation of freedom comes, in Mullahy's terms, when he refuses to be "determined by the requirements and conditions of his own nature," or as Ursinus put it, when he refuses to act in accordance

[13] Heppe, *op.cit.*, p. 244.
[14] Patrick Mullahy, "Will, Choice and Ends," *Psychiatry*, Vol. XII (November, 1949), pp. 383-84.

with the order congruent to his own nature. He vitiates his enjoyment of "the good things suited" to his nature, and chooses, instead, to assume "defects and burdens not proper" to his nature. Thus, in refusing to be less than God, Satan refuses to express himself, and all good to him becomes bane (ix, 122-23), in himself and in others. His pride—the denial of his created nature and the replacement of it by an image of unconditioned deity in his view of himself—he refuses to repudiate, so that repentance is impossible (iv, 98-101). The result is summarized in his admission that, even while he is being "adored" on the throne of infernal divinity, "the lower still I fall, only supreme In misery" (iv, 91-92). Misery is the only absolute which he can achieve for himself.

His self-imposed misery is at union with the self-chosen denial of his own nature. Having abandoned his true being, he becomes the continuous poseur, forever striking attitudes and pretentious postures. He affects the role of liberator, of deliverer from oppressive tyranny, but the freedom he offers to others is the freedom to be enslaved to himself. Only Sin and Death are freed by Satan to act in full accord with their natures, but this liberation represents only the freedom to destroy other selves, the freedom to digest all other life, to incorporate, to extend the demonic possession of life.

Milton personifies Sin and Death as the unnatural products of the Satanic repudiation of nature and of nature's Creator. Sin comes first, the realization of a nightmare, springing fullgrown from Satan's head at the moment when he was plotting the usurpation of deity. She is the "perfect image" (ii, 764) of Satan, combining in herself the fascination of repulsion-attraction, and inciting her father to the incestuous union which bears fruit in the birth of Death. She is "Sin" in the singular, and not "sins," thus representing the essential repudiation of creatureliness, and the disavowal of love and harmony under God. She can in no way be regarded as personifying the violation of particular cultural mores and morals. She is a pseudo-creation, the product of the repudiation of creation proper, and is creation's antagonist.

The union of Satan and Sin brings forth Death—Sin calls him "grim Death my son and foe" (ii, 804)—a shapeless monster, a "vast unhide-bound corpse" (x, 601), whose sport is the rape of his mother, more "inflam'd with lust than rage," (ii, 791) though both lust and rage are patently involved. The fruits of this second incest are the hell hounds. Sin describes how Death

> . . . overtook his mother all dismay'd
> And in embraces forcible and foul
> Ingend'ring with me, of that rape begot
> These yelling monsters that with ceaseless cry
> Surround me, as thou saw'st, hourly conceiv'd
> And hourly born, with sorrow infinite
> To me, for when they list into the womb
> That bred them they return, and howl and gnaw
> My bowels, their repast; then bursting forth
> Afresh with conscious terrors vex me round,
> That rest or intermission none I find. (ii, 792-802)

In the genius of that depiction, we see the horrible return of sin upon itself. In this way, Sin brings forth "sins" at the instance of Death. These two personifications are inseparably bound together, producing the myriad violations of order and harmony which are symbolized by the offal-eating hell hounds. The insatiable anxiety of Death seeks satisfaction in the lust-hate union with Sin, and brings forth a yelping army of new horrors.

To these two distorted "odious offspring" (ii, 781) of his own self-love, Satan gives "freedom" (ii, 822) to enjoy a gluttonous ingorging of human life on earth, where he promises them that "all things shall be your prey" (ii, 844). It is the only promise he ever keeps.

Upon Satan's seduction of man, Sin and Death build a highway of easy access from hell to earth, "a passage broad, Smooth, easy, inoffensive down to hell" (x, 304-5), and prepare to enter upon their new realms. Together the three incestuous figures will preside as an unholy trinity (another demonic aping and perversion of the divine economy) over "one realm, Hell and this world, one realm, one continent Of easy thoroughfare" (x, 391-93). Sin and Death proceed to earth as Satan's plenipotentiaries, to enthrall and destroy. The forces of anti-creation have reached the height of their drive for power and the depth of their departure from love.

IV. THE SATANIC ACHIEVEMENT

By his self-assertive efforts, Satan achieves existence in hell. In hating God, the ground of his own being, and creation, of which he is a part, Satan inevitably puts a curse on himself (iv, 71-72). In this way comes the striking degeneration of the demons. On the fiery lake of hell, Satan scarcely recognizes the once resplendent Beelzebub: "O how fall'n! how chang'd From him, who in the happy realms of light Cloth'd with transcendent brightness didst outshine Myriads though bright" (I, 84-87). Similarly, Satan himself is unrecognizable by Ithuriel and Zephron in the garden, even when he returns from the form of a toad to his own likeness. When alone, Satan admits his degeneration (IX, 487-88), but his sorrow does not stop him from furthering the purposes which brought it on; he appears in the even lower forms of vulture, cormorant, lion, tiger, toad, and serpent. The highest pitch of self-pity comes when he concludes that he must enter the serpent to accomplish the betrayal of man, and so be constrained "into a beast, and mixt with bestial slime, This essence to incarnate and imbrute" (IX, 165-66). Here is perhaps the most striking irony of the life of Antichrist, filled as it is with perverse opposites to the life of the Messiah: the demonic has its own form of incarnation—bestial, not humane, and with the object of securing man's subjection rather than his liberation, his death rather than his life. This preoccupation with domination and death is of the essence of hell.

In the Reformed tradition which forms the general background for Milton's work, hell was regarded not as a geographical area, but as a permanent cast of mind. It exists wherever the Satanic idol is accepted, that is, wherever the wholeness of God is rejected in favor of a lesser good or a positive evil. And the lesser good becomes a positive evil whenever it assumes its own supremacy. "The mind is its own place," Satan declaims in hell, "and in itself Can make a heav'n of hell, a hell of heaven" (i, 254-55). Satan here tells half the truth, for the self-deification of mind can make a hell of heaven, though not a heaven of hell. Elsewhere, when he is alone, Satan speaks the whole truth, declares that he carries torment within him (IX, 120-21), that "which way I fly is hell; myself am hell," (IV, 75) and Milton comments that "from hell One step no more than from himself" can Satan fly by change of place (IV, 21-22) for hell "always in him burns, Though in mid heav'n" (IX, 467-68). While heaven is personal existence forever in the love of God and of God's creatures, hell is existence in the love of Satan.

The fires and other torments of hell are metaphors representing the anguish of chosen isolation from God. "It is not a question of a real fire," Calvin emphatically declares, as he treats the Biblical images of the lot of the damned, whose "anguish and torment are figuratively represented to us under corporeal images."[15] The damned endure hell because they "prefer to perish with Satan,"[16] and the resulting self-chosen alienation from God is what Calvin means by hell, "which is figuratively represented by fire and brimstone,"[17] to convey the utter abysmal lostness and misery of the creature who has separated himself from existence in the love of God. Upon the dissolution of community with God, all community is dissolved, so that hell, "the death of the soul," "is to be without God, to be forsaken by God, to be

[15] *Institutes*, trans. Allen, III, xxv, 12, and Quistorp, *op.cit.*, p. 187.
[16] Quistorp, *ibid.*, p. 190.
[17] John T. McNeill, *The History and Character of Calvinism* (New York: Oxford University Press, 1954), p. 210.

abandoned to oneself."[18] It is, in Karl Barth's words, "a state of exclusion from God, and that makes death so fearful, makes hell what it is. That man is separated from God means being in the place of torment. . . . Godlessness is existence in hell."[19]

Milton describes hell as "a universe of death. . . . Where all life dies, death lives" (II, 622-24). It is, in summary, the seat of sterile power, totally divorced from love; it is the bond of hate, the repudiation of harmonious life, the impossible exaltation of the self-deified self, and the condition of finding joy only in destruction. It is the attempt to have "heaven" without God, and the repudiation of divine love without which all personal integrity becomes fragment and decay. It is, above all, Satan's free gift to man.

[18] Quistorp, *op.cit.*, p. 75.
[19] *Outline*, p. 118.

3

MAN: THE DENIAL OF HUMANITY

I. THE INTEGRITY OF MAN

MAN'S FALL directly parallels that of Lucifer. Repudiating the light which he himself bore as son of morning and prince of light, Lucifer sought to usurp the glory of God. He achieved only darkness, for, as a creature, his power over his destiny could only preserve or destroy himself; it did not include the capacity either to make or to remake himself. The same applies to man, "affecting godhead and so losing all," as God the Father says (III, 206).

Like the Satanic angels, man was created to stand in personal integrity, to exist within a structure of the free realization of his own, but not another's potential. His chief end is declared by Raphael to be that "which best may serve To glorify the Maker, and infer Thee also happier" (VII, 115-17). Governed in freedom by his own choice of love and reason, man was made "sufficient to have stood, though free to fall" (III, 99). Such was God's respect for man's integrity.

But man, too, must respect his own integrity. As his fall came through improper self-assertion, so the continuance of his integrity could only be through proper self-respect. Raphael makes this clear when he says that

> Oft-times nothing profits more
> Than self-esteem, grounded on just and right
> Well manag'd. (VIII, 571-73)

The direction given to human life is within human choice. As Eve tells the serpent, "we live Law to ourselves, our reason is our law" (IX, 653-54). So long as man respects his own existence, he is safe. As Adam most memorably puts it, "within himself The danger lies, yet lies within his power: Against his will he can receive no harm" (IX, 348-50).

There is always the possibility of evil. Without this possibility, man would exist as an object, not as a person, an "it" rather than an "I." If the possibility of the fall were to be made an impossibility, says God the Father, then as God he "must change their [human] nature" (III, 125-26). For God to do this would be, in effect, to ordain for man a fall far more drastic than that which man ordains for himself. It would be to "objectify" man, to reduce him to the stature of a slave. In the words of God the Father, "I form'd them free, and free they must remain, Till they enthrall themselves" (III, 124-25). Here is a freedom which God does not violate, which man can violate, and which Satan, by his own chosen self-deification, will violate.

Another mark of the divine respect for man's integrity is in the establishment of what Adam calls "pleasant labor," the task of tending the universe as a garden within the harmony of God:

> Man hath his daily work of body or mind
> Appointed, which declares his dignity,

And the regard of heav'n on all his ways;
While other animals unactive range,
And of their doing God takes no account,
     (IV, 618-22)

This labor is not for "irksome toil, but to delight" (IX, 242), as Adam tells Eve, and it is only after the fall that it becomes irksome toil, in sorrow and sweat of brow. As the Satanic hosts sought heaven without God and transformed their existence into hell, so man, seeking to be super-human, transforms the human dignity of labor into a curse, a function of the larger alienations of human life.

Man's rule over creation is a mark of the image of God, for his rule is to be in harmony and love. It is significant that Adam gives names to all earthly creatures, thereby indicating his sovereignty, but that he instinctively asks the name of his Creator, revealing the limits of his dominion, the point at which his sovereignty must be caught up in dependence on a larger order of existence. So long as he exists in terms of this dependent sovereignty, all will be well, but his fall from integrity comes precisely at the point where he presumes to assign a name—it is his own name—to deity, and to assume for himself the prerogatives of independent godhead.

In Raphael's direction of Adam's attention towards "which best may serve To glorify the Maker, and infer Thee also happier" (VII, 115-17), the chief goals of human life, God's glory and man's enjoyment, are inseparably united. The latter, as Milton's epic makes clear, is impossible without the former, in which it must be grounded. God made "all things to man's delightful use" (IV, 692), and established the human freedom for happiness: "Happiness in his power left free to will" (V, 235). In this way, man's existence requires community with God. But it requires also community with other men. Man first needs God, and then man, so that after finding his Creator, Adam asks for "human consort: In solitude What happiness, who can enjoy alone, Or all enjoying, what contentment find?" (VIII, 364-66). The Son applauds Adam's recognition that his happiness requires a completion outside itself, finding in it an expression of the "spirit within thee free, My image" (VIII, 440-41). As man is not sufficient in and to himself, as in the sin of the fall he attempts to be, he cannot generate his own completion, but must "sleep" in passivity while it is accomplished for him by his Creator. According to Karl Barth, God "creates not only I and Thou, man and woman, but also their relation to one another as such."[1]

This completion comes partly through sexual love, and it is one of the great Puritan emphases in the Eden saga that sexual love was present in paradise—"the crown of all our bliss," Milton calls it (IV, 728). Of this we shall have more to say later; our present concern is for the manner in which sexual mutuality is the symbol for all mutual dependence in human society. Man cannot exist *as man* in solitude, or in community only with beasts, and it is the work of the image of God that he knows this:

[1] *Barth's Dogmatics*, p. 130.

[45]

> Among unequals what society
> Can sort, what harmony or true delight?
> Which must be mutual, in proportion due
> Giv'n and receiv'd. (VIII, 383-86)

Eve is thus brought both to Adam and from Adam, symbolizing at once the separate individuality of human persons and their inescapable, corporate mutuality. Adam cannot exist alone, and neither can Eve, although she tries to. Telling of her own creation, she recalls how she had been at first enamoured of her own image seen, Narcissus-like, in a smooth lake, until the Creator takes her from communion with shadows to the reality of Adam. To Adam she later says:

> With thee conversing I forget all time,
> All seasons and their change, all please alike,
> Sweet is the breath of morn, her rising sweet,
> With charm of earliest birds; pleasant the sun. . . .
> But neither breath of morn when she ascends
> With charm of earliest birds, nor rising sun,
> On this delightful land, nor herb, fruit, flow'r
> Glist'ring with dew, nor fragrance after showers,
> Nor grateful ev'ning mild, nor silent night
> With this her solemn bird, nor walk by moon,
> Or glittering star-light without thee is sweet.
>   (IV, 639-56)

One of man's earliest discoveries is this need for mutuality. "The structure of man," Reinhold Niebuhr writes, "is such that he cannot complete himself within himself."[2]

---

[2] Reinhold Niebuhr, *Discerning the Signs of the Times* (New York: Charles Scribner's Sons, 1946), p. 90.

Human society expresses man's inner necessity to love and to be loved. Even the angels' joy is in "communion sweet" (v, 637), and Raphael instructs Adam that love "is the scale By which to heav'nly love thou may'st ascend" (VIII, 591-92). Heaven itself is a communion of love, both with God and with other creatures, so that there can be no continued or immortal blessedness for the individual without a continuation of communion with others. The final victory of the divine over the demonic will be the victory of love. This love is linked to reason. In Milton's terms, it interacts with reason, both contributing and receiving, as love "hath its seat In reason" and at the same time "refines the thoughts" (VIII, 589-91). Albert Schweitzer, who has united the life of reason and the life of love as fully as any man in recent centuries, treats the two in much the same fashion as does Milton. "Christianity," he says, "cannot take the place of thinking, but it must be founded on it. . . . I know that I myself owe it to thinking that I was able to retain my faith in religion and in Christianity." At the same time, Schweitzer continues, "the essential element in Christianity as it was preached by Jesus, and as it is comprehended by thought, is this, that it is only through love that we can attain to communion with God. All living knowledge of God rests upon this foundation: that we experience him in our lives as Will-to-Love."[3]

Evil, though primarily an alienation from love, is also a denial of reason. In his very helpful treatment of

[3] Albert Schweitzer, *Out of My Life and Thought*, trans. C. T. Campion (New York: New American Library of World Literature, 1953), p. 184.

human freedom which we noticed in the preceding chapter, Ursinus defined free will as the power of willing or refusing without compulsion "that which the mind dictates as worthy of choice or rejection."[4] In the same vein, Milton writes of original sin that "understanding ruled not, and the will Heard not her lore" (IX, 1127-28). "Reason is our law" (IX, 654), Eve told the serpent, and her sin was in good measure the refusal of reason.

> But God left free the will, for what obeys
> Reason is free, and reason he made right,
> But bid her well beware, and still erect
> Lest by some false appearing good surpris'd
> She dictate false. (IX, 351-55)

This "right reason" is neither an abstract, statemental use of the mind, nor the accumulation of knowledge. It is a fully existential use of the intellect, devoted to temporal choice in terms of everlasting concerns. As it is judgment in accord with the scale of values put into creation by the Creator, it must necessarily be dedicated to love and to freedom, primary values within the created order. Schweitzer's Christian description of thinking, "a harmony within us,"[5] applies both to harmony within the individual and within human society. Thus Nimrod, the tyrant who built the abortive tower of Babel, is said by Michael to have usurped on "rational liberty" (XII, 82), whereas "Discord" is the

---

[4] Heppe, *op.cit.*, p. 244.

[5] Albert Schweitzer, "Religion and Modern Civilization," *The Christian Century*, Vol. LI (November 21, 1934), pp. 1483-84.

first daughter of Sin, placed "among the irrational" (x, 708).

Wisdom is understood in similarly existential terms: "to know That which before us lies in daily life Is the prime wisdom" (vɪɪɪ, 192-94), Milton writes. Like freedom, wisdom may be abandoned, but will not be lost to man except by his own choice: "she deserts thee not, if thou Dismiss not her" (vɪɪɪ, 563-64). Augustine treats wisdom as the true apprehension of the highest good,[6] and although Milton would not deny this meaning to the word, he strongly emphasizes the practical application of it. For Milton, wisdom is the capacity for the best ordering of life, the knowledgeable meeting of immediate needs in terms of everlasting values.

Reason and wisdom, so understood, are clearly distinguished both from speculation[7] and from information. One of the most striking situations in *Paradise Lost* is developed when certain speculative demons in hell

> apart sat on a hill retir'd,
> In thoughts more elevate, and reason'd high
> Of providence, foreknowledge, will, and fate,
> Fixt fate, free will, foreknowledge absolute,
> And found no end, in wand'ring mazes lost.
> Of good and evil much they argu'd then,
> Of happiness and final misery,
> Passion and apathy, and glory and shame.
>   (ɪɪ, 557-64)

[6] *Basic Writings of Saint Augustine*, ed. Whitney J. Oates (New York: Random House, 1948), Vol. ɪ, p. 825, hereafter referred to as *Basic Writings*.

[7] For similar treatments of speculation by Dante, see, for example, *Paradiso*, xɪɪɪ, 114, 118-23, 130-35.

There are few, if any, passages in literature which can surpass the irony of this scene, where the devils debate "final misery" even while they are enduring it. The futility of this endeavor is patent. Milton calls it "vain wisdom all, and false philosophy" (II, 565), for the creatures who practised it used reason not as a device for reestablishing themselves in their full rational freedom, but, rather, as "a pleasing sorcery" to produce "fallacious hope" and "stubborn patience," in obdurate maintenance of the status quo (II, 566-69).

Similarly, wisdom is not meant to be confused with knowledge. Satan tries continually to conflate the two, and to pawn off information as though it were true wisdom. He assures Eve that whoever eats of the tree of knowledge "forthwith attains Wisdom" (IX, 724-25). Milton repeatedly advises "Knowledge within bounds," for

> Knowledge is as food, and needs no less
> Her temperance over appetite, to know
> In measure what the mind may well contain,
> Oppresses else with surfeit, and soon turns
> Wisdom to folly, as nourishment to wind.
>
> (VII, 120-30)

It is well to remember, in reading such passages, that Milton was himself a dedicated intellectual, and probably the last man of whom it could be justly said that he had taken all knowledge for his province. His objection was not to learning as such, but only to learning which "surfeits" the mind, bloats it, makes it unserviceable, and "turns Wisdom to folly." He rigorously insisted on setting bounds to the pursuit of knowledge and of speculation. "Heav'n is for thee too high To know what passes there," Raphael tells Adam. "Be lowly wise: Think only what concerns thee and thy being" (VIII, 172-74).

Man's exaltation of knowledge out of its proper sphere, within the values of creation, parallels his exaltation of himself out of the only order of being in which he can exist in freedom and in joy. God's respect for man's integrity comes in the establishment of love, happiness, liberty, community, reason, and wisdom. Man's proper self-esteem, "grounded on just and right" (VIII, 572), should retain and protect these divinely ordained values, as man lives in respect for God's will and for his own integrity. Man's respect, both for God and himself, should lead him to prize and preserve his own nature, and not to substitute a pseudo-nature, be it a "super-I" or an "it," for his own. In our own time, Schweitzer has expressed the Christian respect for man in his acceptance speech for the Nobel Peace Prize: "The super-man, in the measure that his power increases, becomes himself poorer and poorer. The more we become super-man, the more we become inhuman." In Milton's age, Pascal said it in different, but equally effective, words: "Man is neither angel nor brute, and the unfortunate thing is that he who would act the angel acts the brute."[8]

II. THE ASSUMPTION OF DEITY

The sin of Adam and Eve was repudiating the image of God to attain deity itself. Satan's enticement, from

[8] Blaise Pascal, *Pensées*, trans. W. F. Trotter and Thomas McCrie (New York: Modern Library, 1941), No. 358, p. 118.

the first, was to "be as Gods," to "put on Gods" (ix, 708-14). In the toad-inspired dream, Satan's appeal to Eve is to "be henceforth among the Gods, Thyself a Goddess" (v, 77-78), an appeal he repeats as the serpent urges Eve to be "a Goddess among Gods, ador'd and serv'd" (ix, 547). Adam, too, is not unimpressed by the "serpent's" exaltation to humanity, and unconscious of the irony of seeking "higher degree of life" from the angelic-serpent who had attained only debasement, wishes that he and Eve might "be Gods, or angels demi-Gods" (ix, 934, 937).

The fall came, then, in the quest for deity. The point can hardly be overstressed, for the popular imagination has often insisted upon reading the fall in terms of sensuality, connecting it with the animal instincts in general, and with sexual love in particular. Neither Genesis nor *Paradise Lost* will support such an interpretation. In the religious tradition from which Milton had emerged, John Calvin had called it a "fond and foolish thing" to connect original sin only with the sensual appetites,[9] and he inveighed against the "childish opinion" which regarded it as intemperance.[10] To him, the original sin consisted in the "monstrous impiety that a son of the earth should not be satisfied with being made after the similitude of God, unless he could also be equal to Him."[11] This interpretation represents precisely the position which Milton takes: he makes it impossible to treat the fall as the result of sexual or other

[9] *Institutes*, trans. Norton, ii, i, 9.
[10] *Ibid.*, i, 4.
[11] *Institutes*, trans. Allen, ii, i, 4.

sensuality. Satan's seduction of Eve is not to sex, which she had already known and enjoyed as "the crown of all our bliss" (IV, 728); it is "above" and beyond it, as it is "above" and beyond all of creation. The serpent declares that he had "apprehended nothing high" before eating the fruit, "nor aught but food discern'd Or sex" (IX, 573-74). Seeking to lead Eve to repudiate her natural place in the created order, he belittles sex at the very outset.

Milton ridicules the "hypocrites" who "austerely talk of purity" and malign physical love, "Defaming as impure what God declares Pure, and commands to some, leaves free to all" (IV, 744-47). As to Adam and Eve, Milton leaves no doubt that the fall was far from representing the discovery of physical love. Actually, Adam and Eve seem from the first to have enjoyed the

> Perpetual fountain of domestic sweets
> Whose bed is undefil'd and chaste pronounc't. . . .
> And on their naked limbs the flow'ry roof
> Show'r'd roses, which the morn repair'd. Sleep on,
> Blest pair; and O yet happiest if ye seek
> No happier state, and know to know no more.
>
> (IV, 760-61, 772-75)

It is not to this that Satan incites man. Indeed, Milton says, it is one of the demonic functions to attack conjugal love: "who bids abstain But our destroyer, foe to God and man?" (IV, 748-49) What comes to Adam and Eve in the lustful orgy after the fall is a caricature of the earlier love, when they had been "imparadis't in one another's arms" (IV, 506), "the loveliest pair That ever since in love's embraces met" (IV, 321-22). The first "agony of love" comes with the fall, "till now Not felt," Eve says (IX, 858-59), as she shares in Satan's own substitution for love of "fierce desire" which "still unfulfill'd with pain of longing pines" (IV, 509-11). Thus Adam and Eve arise from their post-lapsarian intercourse not united, but divided and alienated.

Satan's appeal to Eve is not that she should be natural, but rather that she should be super-natural, and her fall comes in attempting to ascend. In doing so, she moves through the four clearly defined stages into which sin was analyzed in Milton's age. First, there is suggestion, Satan's persuasive proffer of the fruit and of its promised results. Next comes delectation, a mental tasting, an imaginary revelling in the suggested sin and its enjoyment. Then there is consent—"Here grows the cure of all, this fruit divine" (IX, 776)—and, finally, the actual commission. The first stage, suggestion, was innocent, for it was presented externally to the mind; as Adam had earlier explained to Eve the temptation of her dream, evil in this fashion may "come and go," if it is unapproved, and "leave No spot or blame behind" (V, 117-19). Eve's approval became partial in delectation, full in consent, and was finally sealed in action.

Adam's fall follows the same general pattern, though with important differences at each stage, as he moves more deliberately and more knowingly. He, too, is thinking of deity, but in addition to "affecting Godhead" (III, 206) he also takes Eve as his "god." At least in part, his is a genuine love of Eve as a lesser good, directed not to the Creator but to the creature, not to the giver but to the gift. In Augustine's terms, his choice is to love and serve the creature rather than the Creator[12] and he makes communion with Eve the grounds of his happiness. By choice, his chief end is now the association with Eve rather than with God, the choice of a mutable life rather than life itself. Thus he consents to eat, for "if death Consort with thee, death is to me as life" (IX, 953-54). As Satan had chosen evil for his good, so now Adam chooses death as his life.

The fall is now complete. Man has chosen an arbitrary knowledge of good and evil over the freedom of his own being under God: he has made himself the creator of ethical absolutes, the maker of norms, and the judge of his own actions. Man is the measure, the measurer, and, inevitably, the measured, as well. In choosing to be super-human, he has purchased the super-ego with the price of free life. Man makes man his own god, himself the ultimate source of his own well being and beatitude, and the result is enslavement. "Whether he will or no," as Augustine has it, "a man is necessarily a slave to the things by means of which he seeks to be happy. He follows them whithersoever they lead, and fears anyone who seems to have the power to rob him of them."[13]

III. THE CONTEST OF GODS

By the revolt from God, man separates himself from the only being to whom wholeness adheres. As a creature, he exalts himself into the role of his own god, and seeks, in allegiance to himself, the ground of his in-

[12] *Earlier Writings*, p. 259.
[13] *Ibid.*, p. 260.

tegrity. But the human integer, along with all created and derivative life, can maintain wholeness only by maintaining a common allegiance to the source of all integrity. In the fall, men rebel as parts against unity and, in consequence, become isolated and antagonistic fragments. Thus when the Son found Adam and Eve in the garden after the fall, "love was not in their looks, either to God Or to each other" (x, 111-12). As we shall later comment, this lovelessness implies, in general, a threefold isolation: from God, from themselves, and from each other. Let us first observe in the fall several more particular results.

Immediately after eating the fruit which was to make her divine, Eve proceeds to worship the tree as though it were itself divine. Not only has she usurped divinity, but she has conferred it upon the tree which will now, she says, receive the morning worship formerly directed to God:

> . . . henceforth my early care,
> Not without song, each morning, and due praise
> Shall tend thee. (IX, 799-801)

Before she leaves to seek for Adam, she makes a low genuflection before the tree "as to the power That dwelt within" (IX, 835-36) and then passes on. She becomes less than she had been, because, as Augustine said of Satan, she "wished to enjoy what was less."[14] And God allows her to have her wish.

Anxiety comes immediately. "But to Adam" she asks, "in what sort Shall I appear?" (IX, 816-17) Tension seizes

[14] *Ibid.*, p. 237.

her as she envisions separation from him and envies the
new "Eve" who will replace her. Her love for Adam
is now a form of self-love, so that the separation from
him which she dreads is already a present reality. Less
interested in Adam than in exercising power over him,
Eve would "Keep the odds of knowledge in my power
Without copartner" (IX, 820-21); nonetheless, she deter-
mines to offer him the fruit out of envy for a continued
happiness from which she would be excluded—"a death
to think" (IX, 830), she calls it. The future holds
nothing but anxiety in her present thoughts, for death
is already upon her, although Milton, with characteristic
irony, has her ask "what if God have seen And death
ensue?" (IX, 826-27)

Meeting Adam, she now begins her deceitful appeal
to him. She not only persuades him to accept what she
herself believes, that the tree can "make them Gods
who taste" (IX, 866) but also beguiles him, and perhaps
herself as well, with the false appeal that it was chiefly
for him that she had sought divinity. She proceeds to a
direct contradiction of her own admitted unwillingness
that Adam should live without her, an anxiety which
overcame her desire to retain the "power" of her new
estate, as she assures Adam that she would die alone and
in misery before she would cause his death:

> Were it I thought Death menac't would ensue
> This my attempt, I would sustain alone
> The worst, and not persuade thee, rather die
> Deserted, than oblige thee with a fact
> Pernicious to thy peace. . . . (IX, 977-81)

Actually, as we have seen, it was precisely the thought of her own death, and Adam's peace in the enjoyment of another Eve, which led her to accept him as her "co-partner" (ix, 821). But Eve now regards herself as a god, and so makes and unmakes truth and falsehood to suit her purposes.

Adam accepts her own evaluation, and places his faith, hope, and love in the creature, to the direct exclusion of the Creator. The Son later rebukes Adam with the central question, "Was she thy God, that her thou didst obey" (x, 145), to which only one answer can be truthfully returned: for all practical purposes, Adam takes Eve as his god. His faith is explicitly placed in her, in response to her specific appeal for that faith: "On my experience, Adam, freely taste, And fear of death deliver to the winds" (ix, 988-89). His hope, again, is in her assurance of "growing up to Godhead," (ix, 877) and his act of eating was a "glorious trial of exceeding love" for her (ix, 961). Adam's whole existence is disorbited by this misplacing of the theological virtues. Eve has achieved her godhead over Adam, though only for a brief moment.

Both having asserted divinity, difficulties arise almost immediately, as they inevitably become not copartners, but rivals. Which god is supreme? Which god is to judge? Which god is to give way? With the love of the supreme God lost, no ground is left for reconciliation, and Adam and Eve now exist in their own self-assertions of independent godhood. Adam is as much a god as Eve, and what had once been the glorious trial of his exceeding love for her gives place to the contest of competing recriminations. Each judges the other, shame is introduced (IX, 1097), and fig leaves are taken as a covering to their guilt and as a badge of their division, a seal placed on the destruction of mutuality.

In the words of God and man alike, the result of the fall is the knowledge of "good lost, and evil got" (IX, 1072 and XI, 87). Like the destroyer whose lead they followed, men now "saw undelighted all delight" (IV, 286). Sleep becomes unrest, love an agony, and "just confidence" (IX, 1045-98) is exchanged for inner torments:

> high winds worse within
> Began to rise, high passions, anger, hate,
> Mistrust, suspicion, discord, and shook sore
> Their inward state of mind, calm region once
> And full of peace, now toss't, and turbulent.
>   (IX, 1122-26)

Subject now, like Satan, to "the hateful siege Of contraries" (IX, 121-22), man finds that an innocent joy in the good works of nature gives way to an evil shame, "honor dishonorable" (IV, 314), as Adam and Eve withdraw into themselves and would even abandon themselves entirely.

IV. ALIENATION AND ISOLATION

The results for Adam and Eve are alienation and isolation. The alienation is from God, from themselves, and from each other; and the concomitant isolation represents torment because it is isolation with a self which is alienated from itself. Calvin's words aptly describe the situation of this death of the soul, which is "to be without God . . . to be abandoned to oneself."[15]

The fall, when treated in these terms, has three facets: the alienation from God, from self, and from other selves. Adam first recognizes the separation from God (what Cocceius called the fall from God's friendship)[16] and he cries out

> How shall I behold the face
> Henceforth of God or angel, erst with joy
> And rapture so oft beheld? (IX, 1080-82)

Thus when the Son comes into the garden, Adam and Eve hide themselves from him, seeking to cut themselves off from him by sheltering themselves among "the thickest trees" (X, 101) just as they cut themselves off from each other by the shelter of leaves from the fruitless fig tree (IX, 1100-14).

The second alienation is from themselves, that is, Adam from Adam, Eve from Eve. Inner tempests arise to shake the once calm region of the mind (IX, 1122-26). The rule of conscience as a free inward guide is lost, and conscience becomes instead an inner fear, out of which man can "find no way, from deep to deeper plung'd" (X, 844). Right reason is overthrown, the "understanding rul'd not" (IX, 1127), and as Augustine put it, man's usurpation upon God has led him to know "by suffering" the evil he had not mastered by avoiding it.[17] The result is a knowledge of evil which is not external, but now inwardly felt in pain and anguish.

---

[15] Quistorp, *op.cit.*, p. 75.
[16] Heppe, *op.cit.*, p. 311.
[17] *Earlier Writings*, p. 243.

Although Adam and Eve judge sin itself less severely than God judges it, they judge themselves far more severely than God judges them. Totally lost to them now is that proper "self-esteem, grounded on just and right Well manag'd" (VIII, 572-73), which Raphael had advised; replacing it is self-contempt and the wish for annihilation. Even the death wish, however, is not free from fear and pain, but is clearly the product of self-hate. In his long and agonizing self-examination, Adam accuses God of creating him without his consent, and even when he accepts God's justice it is without love for God or for himself. He sees only God's power, not his love, only the divine hatred of sin, not the divine love for the sinful creature, and speaks much as did Martin Luther when he declared that "I did not love a just and angry God, but rather hated and murmured against him."[18] Fearful of God, in revolt against God, repudiating himself as he has already repudiated God, wishing for the death he fears, Adam exists "in a troubl'd sea of passion toss't" (X, 718).

In addition to the alienation from God and from the self, there is also, in Adam and Eve, the alienation from each other. The result of self-deification is isolation, as each of the rival gods both judges and excludes, and is judged and excluded by the other. This mutual recrimination exists openly with the inward self-alienation which both feel, but neither will confess to the other:

[18] Roland H. Bainton, *Here I Stand, A Life of Martin Luther* (New York: Abingdon Press, 1950), p. 65.

Thus they in mutual accusation spent
The fruitless hours, but neither self-condemning,
And of their vain contest appear'd no end. (IX, 1187-89)

The mutuality in which man was created is destroyed.

Karl Barth's interpretation of the image of God with which the Genesis saga endows man is quite revealing and suggestive here.[19] Barth interprets this image as an analogy of relationship, the inescapable mutuality of male and female. The fall is a breaking of all human relationships as symbolized in this one facet of mutuality; it is the destruction of human community, the alienation of man from his fellows. God is replaced by gods, engaged in passing judgment on each other within a rivalry of pretension. The result of self-deification is isolation, the loss of community between men, as well as the loss of communion with God.

V. THE COURSE OF TIME

We have already indicated that our treatment of Milton's epic would be in terms of the doctrine of accommodation, so important in the Reformation, and in terms of the modern theologians' understanding of the Genesis stories as saga, poetry and parable. The events treated are not "history" in a chronological sense, but are trans-historical, as they furnish an insight into all history. Creation and fall are the foundation of history, not in a temporal, but in an existential manner. The elemental scheme of human existence is depicted in the

[19] *Barth's Dogmatics*, pp. 125-26.

life of Adam, the Hebrew *adham*, man, or Everyman. This Adam is representative of all men, the combining or federal symbol of the entire human race, the summarizing figure of every human creature in chosen isolation from God. What happens to Adam, as Milton dramatizes it in detail, is repeated in the succession of parabolic and factual events seen from the mount of vision in the last two books of the epic. Thus it is that the fall of Everyman is seen as the continuous fact of human history. The pleasant and graceful labor of tending the earth as a garden gives place to the anxiety of living by the sweat of the brow in Satan's "perverted world" (XII, 547). Power succeeds upon love, and, as it does so, the next successive result within the saga is Cain's murder of Abel. The fatherhood of God having been repudiated, fratricide replaces brotherhood (XI, 455-57). Violence, oppression and "sword-law" (XI, 672) are exalted, as Satan's demonic view of war and slaughter, which he styles "the strife of glory" (VI, 290), becomes the governing order of human relations:

> Might only shall be admir'd,
> And Valor and heroic Virtue call'd;
> To overcome in battle, and subdue
> Nations, and bring home spoils with infinite
> Man-slaughter, shall be held the highest pitch
> Of human glory: and for glory done,
> Of triumph, to be styl'd great conquerors,
> Patrons of mankind, gods, and sons of gods,
> Destroyers rightlier call'd and plagues of men.
>   (XI, 689-97)

As the Satanic perversion spreads throughout human society, the greatest "glory" of man is seen in destruction and the force of war, as man, patterning himself on the image of the demonic rather than the divine, "to glory aspires Vain-glorious, and through infamy seeks fame" (vi, 383-84). Continually violating the mutuality of human creation, "a world devote to universal rack" (xi, 821) exalts its own destroyers, the perverters of its peace, and wildly glorifies its fiercest members:

> Death's ministers, not men, who thus deal death
> Inhumanly to men, and multiply
> Ten thousandfold the sin of him who slew
> His brother. (xi, 676-79)

Death, the "vast unhidebound corpse" (x, 601), sprung in distortion from the incestuous union of Satan with his own nightmare, now rules in ravin over all the earth.

But war is not the only evil, for peace is found "to corrupt no less than war to waste" (xi, 784), as men, disorbited from their true center, flounder in their attempts to establish themselves as gods without God. Tyrants arise who, even in peace, take men and beasts alike to be their game (xii, 30), and subdue their brethren in the endless exercise of usurped and pseudo-godlike sovereignty. Of Nimrod, Adam bitterly cries out:

> O execrable son so to aspire
> Above his brethren, to himself assuming
> Authority usurpt, from God not giv'n:
> He gave us only over beast, fish, fowl
> Dominion absolute; that right we hold

By his donation; but man over men
He made not Lord; such title to himself
Reserving, human left from human free.
  (XII, 64-71)

Having first usurped upon God, man has usurped the
only legitimate power over man, and inevitably enslaves
his fellows. This usurpation is both secular, under the
power of tyrants, and sacred, under the power of priests,
who not only take upon themselves arbitrament over
kings and rulers but, in the Christian era, will be found
"to themselves appropriating The Spirit of God,
promis'd alike and giv'n To all believers" (XII, 518-20).
The twin usurpations over the two realms of state and
church are essentially one, stemming from the central
and primary sin of self-deification.

In direct antithesis to the power of God, which unites
man in free community, the power of a sheer humanism
divides. Among the extensions of the parable of the fall
which Milton shows from the mount of vision, none is
more impressive than the story of the tower of Babel
and the origin of different languages. The purpose of
the Babylonians was to build a seat of absolute security,
a tower "whose top may reach to heav'n" (XII, 44), a
city worthy of their pretensions. The action was the
product of anxiety lest "their memory be lost" (XII, 46),
based on the faith that their name was worth preserving
"regardless whether good or evil fame" (XII, 47), and
the material used for constructing the tower which was
to reach to the very realm of God was "a black bitumi-
nous gurge" (XII, 41), boiling out from the mouth of
hell. Founded by presumption, and built with the mat-

ter of hell to be a memorial of power, the effort falls to confusion when tongues descend on the builders, separate them from each other, and divide man from man. The whole parabolic incident stands as a sort of Pentecost in reverse, an extension rather than an eradication of the fall.

VI. THE RETURN TO EARTH

Let us now return from the story of humanity to the life of the archetypal Everyman. To trace the transhistorical significance of the primary sin through history, as Milton unfolds it on the mount of vision, we have temporarily bypassed some of the most important pages of Adam's story. We left that story at the point of man's threefold alienation—from God, from himself, and from human community. Finding himself unable to restore wholeness to any of these relationships, Adam responds to his impasse with the wish for death. Eve carries this response to its logical conclusion, and suggests that they actively seek death. Destruction is the patent result of their transgression, as all their joys have been betrayed even in life, and "destruction with destruction to destroy" (x, 1006) is Eve's only vision of escape. As wholeness is unattainable, then the fragments should refuse to continue themselves. Two alternatives come to Eve's mind: she suggests that escape may be found either through genocide or suicide, through total abstinence from procreation or the cancelling out of their own existence.

Although both courses represent forms of self-denial

based in morbidity, the background out of which these proposals grow is hopeful. Adam, having cursed Eve as the serpent, has been moved by her plea to him for reconciliation, and by her prayer to heaven that all the punishment may light on her head alone, as she accepts sole responsibility for the evil which they have together committed (x, 935). Adam, under the impact of this gesture of love, turns from bitter recrimination to the wish that "on my head all might be visited" (x, 955), for Eve's sin and his own. Milton says, "Prevenient grace descending had remov'd The stony from their hearts" (xi, 3-4), so that by the free mercy of God they were able to turn. These are the fruits, the Son says to the Father, which spring from "thy seed Sown with contrition" (xi, 26-7) in man's heart. What had been mere attrition, mere masochistic and sadistic remorse, is now converted into true penitence. In striking contrast to the fallen angels, both Adam and Eve are now willing to bring more pain on themselves, if only each could thereby deliver the other from pain.

Actually they go further, and would dissipate the entire entail of evil upon themselves in order to spare the human race. "O were I able To waste it all myself," says Adam, and leave none for others to suffer (x, 819-20), while Eve bewails the "wretched life" which comes as the result of sin, and declares "miserable it is To be to others cause of misery" (x, 981-85). For Satan, the spread of misery is the only source of joy, "for only in destroying I find ease" (ix, 129). Here the contrast between fallen man and fallen angel is most sharp, and most decisive. The difference between these statements

precisely marks the distance separating sinful and penitent man from presumptuous and impenitent devil, and
underscores the limitations of grace. Man is defrauded,
but Satan is fraud itself.

Although Eve's suggestion of ending the entail of
misery by suicide or by genocide is a product of this
great mark of her distinction from Satan, it also indicates
the limits of her sinful nature. As she cannot elevate herself by her own act of self-affirmation, neither can she
redeem herself by her own self-negation. The particular
forms of self-denial which come to her mind are only
more subtle forms of self-centeredness, of anguish and
regret, rather than full penitence, as Adam points out
(x, 1016-19). She is still acting as her own judge, her
own god. Redemption can only come, Adam tells Eve,
in the judgment of God. Man can judge himself no
more properly than he can judge another. The proper
submission for man is not to himself but to God, and
Adam sees in the judgment of the Son a union of
promise with sentence, of deliverance with punishment.
It is only in the acceptance of this divine sovereignty—
"Remember with what mild And gracious temper he
both heard and judg'd Without wrath or reviling" (x,
1046-48)—that true self-denial is possible, a self-denial
which is at once self-respect. What man must deny in
himself is the urge to make himself a god, and this he
cannot deny so long as he treats himself both as rebellious sinner and as divine judge. He must escape from
his own judgment as well as from his own sin, and this
he can do only through reconciliation with God,

... in whose look serene,
When angry most he seem'd and most severe,
What else but favor, grace, and mercy shone?
    (x, 1094-96)

The most that man can do to close the breach of his fall is to pray for forgiveness and reinstatement. So Adam and Eve, repairing to the place of their judgment and, as it were, founding their hope upon their sentence, pray "from hearts contrite" (x, 1103). The tragic chapter which began with the desire for divine wings "where-with to scorn the earth" (x, 1011) ends in prostration on the very earth they had scorned, in humble penitence before the God whom they had denied.

GOD: THE PLAN OF SALVATION

I. MAN'S PROBLEM BEFORE GOD

FACED WITH THE CHRISTIAN VIEW of man's situation, non-Christians are sometimes inclined to suggest that if God is omnipotent creator and ruler, then he must bear the responsibility for man's depravity and should, therefore, bear the burden for it. Christians, on the other hand, deny that God bears the responsibility for man's guilt, but declare that he does indeed bear the burden for that guilt. The responsibility is with men, for God "form'd them free, and free they must remain, Till they enthrall themselves" (III, 124-25), but the guilt is assumed by the Son, who became "mortal to redeem Man's mortal crime" (III, 214-15), and who endured the punishment which he had himself placed upon man's sin, reconciling and reinstating man by "coming in the flesh To a reproachful life and cursed death" (XII, 405-6).

It is through this classic pattern that Milton justifies the ways of God to men, and fulfills the purpose to which he dedicated his epic. *Paradise Lost*, as an assertion of eternal providence, of God's reversal of evil, is far less concerned with the commission of sin than with the triumph of grace. God, as we have seen, bears no responsibility for the free choice of a free agent; nonetheless, he bears all the results accruing to the creature that betrayed itself, and he is, in the person of the Son, "slain for bringing life" (XII, 414). The meaning of "grace" may be measured by the difference between the burden borne and the responsibility owed, that is, between all and nothing, so that grace is said to be infinite. It is the free gift of that for which God has no obligation to men, who have no right to demand. Only God can save man from the warping by which he has assumed himself to be a petty divinity.

The process of redemption cannot be understood by setting up a vulgar opposition between the love of the Son and the wrath of the Father, for in the Son "all his Father shone Substantially express'd" (III, 139-40), and in him "the fulness dwells of love divine" (III, 225). The Son is the fullest revelation of the Father, as Milton repeatedly emphasizes, so that we cannot regard the atonement as an independent propitiation of God's hate. Calvin's remarks are suggestive here. He interprets the enmity and wrath of God and "such manner of phrases" as accommodations to our limited capacity, for how otherwise could God be understood to have given us in his Son "a singular pledge of his love"?[1] The significance of the atonement is not the propitiation *of* an angry God, but reconciliation *by* a merciful God. To this point we shall recur in greater detail. Our present concern is with man, who "atonement for himself . . . hath none to bring" (III, 234-35). This point, basic to Christian thought, is inherent in the structure of Milton's epic, and may need some explanation. It is precisely because man needs salvation from himself—from his own self-centeredness—that he cannot, by himself, save himself.

[1] *Institutes,* trans. Norton, II, xvi, 2.

Outward immorality he can indeed combat, and a high degree of civic virtue he may attain, but immorality does not define sin, nor virtue define righteousness. Sin is primarily—"originally"—self-deification, the attempt to warp all life, and all that lives, into one's own orbit. It is the reduction of all things to one's own dominion, the exaltation of the self above all else. It is the manner in which man is enslaved to himself, to his own ultimacy. From this slavery there can be rescue, but no escape.

Man's very efforts at salvation fortify the way against escape from his own prison. His attempts at self-improvement are, in varying degrees of overtness or subtlety, attempts at self-satisfaction, and the most stringent ethics become the clothing for self-righteous gratification, whether on a naive or sophisticated level. Thus man's greatest virtues become, as Augustine said, the most splendid vices. Neither the servile effort to please God by good works so as to extort from him a celestial reward, nor the devotion to good works because man rewards himself for them with a rosy glow of self-satisfaction, will suffice for salvation here or hereafter. Men are in a much more serious predicament. They must "renounce Their own both righteous and unrighteous deeds," and, as God the Father says to the Son, "live in thee transplanted, and from thee Receive new life" (IV, 291-94).

Man's rescue comes when he accepts God's acceptance of him, his reconciliation by the Son, and the end of his threefold alienation. This is the meaning of faith, what Cranmer called "a sure trust and confidence in God's merciful promises . . . whereof doth follow a loving

heart to obey his commandments."[2] Faith, understood
in the sense of the Reformation fathers, is not an assent
to propositions, but a reliance in confidence, a recognition of reconciliation, and an acceptance of life now
orbited on the center of God, rather than self. Faith is
not an affirmation made with gritted teeth, it is not a
"work" of the self-assertive man. "Indeed," as Frans
Burmann had it, "faith is so opposed to works in this
manner that it even excludes itself, if it is considered as
a work."[3] Faith is passive: in one sense it is a kind of
vessel into which God's reconciliation is poured.

Such faith abrogates the sin of self-improvement,
which is but a more subtle form of the primary sin of
self-deification. Donald Baillie, the eminent Scot who
has written the finest modern treatise on the incarnation, poses the dilemma of moralism in this fashion: "It
seems impossible to change ourselves from being interested mainly in ourselves to being concerned with God
and our fellows, because the more we try, the more are
we concentrating on ourselves. How could we save ourselves *from* ourselves? We need to be drawn *out of* ourselves into the life of unselfish community."[4] In view
of this impasse, it becomes clear what Milton means by
the necessity for man to renounce both his "righteous
and unrighteous deeds" (III, 292). Man cannot escape
from enslavement to his sin. He can only be rescued by

[2] Thomas Cranmer, *Works*, ed. John Edmund Cox (Cambridge: The University Press, 1846), Vol. II, p. 133.

[3] Heppe, *op.cit.*, p. 554.

[4] Donald M. Baillie, *God Was In Christ, An Essay on Incarnation and Atonement* (New York: Charles Scribner's Sons, 1948),
p. 206.

the initiative of God, and presented with freedom as a gift. That is the work of the Incarnation.

In treating this problem of man's impasse, Martin Luther recalls Horace's rule of dramatic art, that a god must not be brought into the action until it has become so ensnarled that only a god could unravel it. And, Luther adds, the human drama has reached that point. Only God can provide the denouement.[5]

II. THE WORK OF THE SON

According to Milton's epic of the Genesis saga, man begins by standing on his own mutable goodness, from which he can fall at any time by his own choice, for the results are consequent entirely upon his own action. The fall itself, however, is not merely tragic, because the earlier human mutability is now replaced by an unbreakable divine promise of grace. The second state of man is now happier than the first, for it depends fully and only on God. Milton knows nothing of divine reprobation, by which some men are passed over and left to their damnation by God, and he has no place for a "double decree" of predestination to be damned. God the Father emphatically declares that not only the saved but also "the rest shall hear me call," and none "from mercy I exclude" (III, 185, 202) except those who wilfully refuse the divine reconciliation; that is to say, only those are excluded who exclude themselves. Those who accept rescue will be upheld by God, and their lives will become a process of growth:

[5] Baillie, *ibid.*, p. 171.

Light after light well us'd they shall attain,
And to the end persisting, safe arrive. (III, 196-97)

The anxiety produced by sin and death is no more, and the death of fear is one of the preludes to the death of Death itself, as the divine promise has revealed. Release from the fear of death is one of the principal liberties conferred by the new convenant, for, as Cocceius put it, Christian *libertas* is "the opposite of the fear of death."[6] The faith through which this happier paradise is expressed is not a mere knowledge of the existence of God, but an existential assurance of the love of God, an assurance which comes through a belief in the Messiah. The Son comes "proclaiming life to all who shall believe In his redemption" (XII, 407-8). The belief is that "His merits [will] save them" (XII, 409-10), where their own can not. In this faith, man accepts the fact that he has been accepted by God.

The Son is the ultimate accommodation of the divine to human need and understanding, the final and unique culmination of all the lesser accommodations we have noticed. He is the self-expression, the self-objectification of God, the supreme gesture by which God introduces himself to man. Of the Son, Milton says that "he all his Father full exprest" (VI, 720), and "in him all his Father shone Substantially express'd" (III, 139-40), "whom else no creature can behold" (III, 387).* The Son primarily

[6] Heppe, *op.cit.*, p. 404.

* Except for a footnote explaining that I did not regard *Paradise Lost* as an Arian document, I had planned to omit any reference in my text to Milton's alleged Arianism. Innumerable treatises have been written on trinitarianism, on Arianism, and on the relations between them, and it did not seem to the pur-

reveals God in terms of extrinsic love, of love turned outward toward men.

William Temple, the late archbishop of Canterbury, has some remarks here which will expand our understanding of the Son's role. "The ultimate truth about God and his relation to finite spirits is this, that 'when he is reviled he reviles not again, and when he suffers, he threatens not.'[7] Now that is the only possible mode of omnipotence in a world that contains free spirits."[8] Again, if the heart and will of man, that is, man's in-

---

pose to examine the complexities of those relationships here. Milton, in *Paradise Lost*, had not made it necessary that we do so. After having saturated myself in the trinitarian formulations of Protestantism, I was quite convinced that Milton could never be convicted, before a fair and competent theological court, of trinitarian heresy in *Paradise Lost*. I was therefore delighted to find my own judgment independently corroborated after the completion of this study, but before its publication, by the appearance early in 1959 of "Milton's Arianism Reconsidered," by William B. Hunter, Jr. (*Harvard Theological Review*, Vol. LII, pp. 9-35). Professor Hunter has pursued the complex developments of trinitarian thought with remarkable clarity, and has clearly demonstrated that Milton's theology was not Arian. He has also shown that at other points, Milton's views of the trinity, though differing from those generally held, were not out of keeping either with the Apostles' or the Nicene Creeds, and has traced the primary influences on Milton's trinitarian doctrines to the early Church fathers and to the Bible. In another essay relative to Milton's Christology, which appeared concurrently with Hunter's article, Professor C. A. Patrides demonstrated that Milton's treatment of the Atonement, far from being a merely "personal emphasis," was in the mainstream of Protestant thought ("Milton and the Protestant Theory of the Atonement," *PMLA*, Vol. LXXIV, pp. 7-13).

[7] I Peter 2:23.

[8] William Temple, *William Temple's Teaching*, ed. A. E. Baker (Philadelphia: Westminster Press, 1951), p. 65.

wardness, is to be "won" for God, Temple says it must "be won in such a way that its allegiance was no contradiction of its freedom."[9] It is through the free appeal of love that God seeks to lead man to his proper existence with an inner paradise: thus the work of the Son. At the same time, as Temple puts it, God "knows love to be the best thing there is; therefore, for love's sake, he will be very stern with us when we turn away from that best."[10] This is the metaphor of the anger of God. The two, love and "anger," are linked by God the Father when he declares that all men "shall hear me call," and, at the same time, all shall "oft be warned" (III, 185). They are linked again when the Son judges man with mercy and justice "colleague" (x, 59), offering promise of redemption in the very sentence he imposes. The Atonement, therefore, comes as an appeal to man to love God, rather than for God to love man. It is, indeed, the statement that God *does* love man. The Atonement is God's action, God's decision, and Christ is no humanly-offered sacrifice to appease a remote and merciless God, but, on the contrary, the deity's self-initiated manner of reconciling man to God and to himself.

When Sin is understood in Milton's personification as a malignant force which destroys man's life, turning man over as a prey to Death even while promising to enlarge the existence it destroys, we then see clearly why God, the creator and preserver of all life, must hate and

[9] *Teaching*, p. 65.
[10] Temple, "The Idea of God," *Spectator*, Vol. CXLVI (April 4, 1931), pp. 537-38.

condemn sin precisely because he loves the sinner. His hatred and his love are essentially one, and this oneness underlies both the condemnation of the demonic and the redemption of the human. So it is that, in the Son, mercy becomes "colleague with justice" (x, 59), as the Son's acts "end the strife Of mercy and justice" (III, 406-7). The intellectual embarrassment of the apparent contradiction between God's love and God's judgment is overcome, and this, according to Reinhold Niebuhr, is one fundamental significance of the revelation in Christ.[11] The very sentence of Adam and Eve is pronounced by the Son in his dual role of "judge and savior" (x, 209), so that the condemnation itself predicates redemption:

> So spake this oracle, then verifi'd
> When Jesus son of Mary second Eve
> Saw Satan fall like lightning down from heav'n,
> Prince of the air; then rising from his grave
> Spoil'd principalities and powers, triumpht
> In open show, and with ascension bright
> Captivity led captive through the air,
> The realm itself of Satan long usurpt,
> Whom he shall tread at last under our feet,
> Even he who now foretold his fatal bruise.
> (x, 182-91)

The apparent contrast between "judgment" and "forgiveness" in the abstract is dissolved in fact by the action of the Son, in which both are inextricably united.

In the Son's judgment, as Adam later remarks, "when

[11] *op.cit.*, p. 135.

angry most he seem'd and most severe, What else but favour, grace, and mercy shone?" (x, 1095-96). He pronounces sentence "without wrath or reviling," "pitying while he judg'd" (x, 1048, 1059). Of the very penalty which he announces, the fullest measure, "the worst," the Son says, "on me must light" (x, 73), so that he sentences himself in sentencing man. His judgment is such that he himself will bear it. The whole action is a union of condemnation and release, of conviction and satisfaction, of punishment and deliverance, to the end that

> ... no cloud
> Of anger shall remain, but peace assur'd,
> And reconcilement; wrath shall be no more
> Thenceforth, but in thy presence joy entire.
>   (III, 262-65)

In the providence of God, "over wrath grace shall abound" (XII, 478) and "heav'nly love shall outdo hellish hate" (III, 298). The Atonement may be seen in terms of this divine symmetry, in which evil is cancelled out by good. This symmetry of action has the most powerful aesthetic beauty, for as man's fall was through creaturely assault "against the high supremacy of heav'n, Affecting Godhead, and so losing all" (III, 205-6), so his reinstatement is through the divine emptying of the Son, who repudiates the fact that he is "equal to God, and equally enjoying God-like fruition" (III, 306-7) to be a "man among men on earth" (III, 283). The work of the Son precisely reverses, in a gesture of almost mathematical beauty, the thrust of man's self-exaltation to equality with God. It cancels out, as it were, the presumption of Adam's becoming superman. As Barth puts it, the holiness of Jesus, in whom the Son became incarnate, "means that he did not treat his own goodness as an independent thing, a heroic human achievement. His sinlessness consists in his renouncing all claim to ethical heroism. . . . The God-Man is the only man who claims nothing for himself, but all for God."[12] Or, as Tillich says, Jesus is the Christ because he "sacrifices what is merely 'Jesus' in him."[13] Milton has the Son declare to the Father that he assumes "scepter and power" so that "in the end Thou shalt be all in all, and I in thee Forever, and in me all whom thou lov'st" (VI, 730-33). To this end, man's very "doom," the Son says, "to better life shall yield him, where with me All my redeem'd may dwell in joy and bliss, Made one with me as I with thee am one" (XI, 40-44).

As the incarnate Son relies not on his own "ethical heroism" but on the Father, whom he alone can see, so the truly emancipated man relies, not on his own self-assertive efforts, but on the incarnate Son, who alone reveals all that man can comprehend of God. In this reliance upon the only merit available to him, man is rescued out of the impasse from which he could not work his own escape. The result is freedom, the only freedom available to man in bondage to his own self-centeredness. In this emancipation the possibility of growth appears, as "light after light well us'd they shall attain" (III, 196), whereas for "those who, when they

---

[12] Baillie, *op.cit.*, p. 127.
[13] *Op.cit.*, Vol. I, p. 134.

may, accept not grace" (III, 302), but repudiate the divine offer, they shall "stumble on, and deeper fall" (III, 201). There is security only in growth, in advance, while growth and advance are possible only through that existential acceptance of God's redemption which is called "belief" or "faith." Michael teaches Adam of the incarnate Son that

> The Law of God exact he shall fulfill
> Both by obedience and by love, though love
> Alone fulfill the law; thy punishment
> He shall endure by coming in the flesh
> To a reproachful life and cursed death,
> Proclaiming life to all who shall believe
> In his redemption, and that his obedience
> Imputed becomes theirs by faith, his merits
> To save them, not their own though legal works.
> (XII, 402-10)

Faith is the existential incorporation of God's redemption, the application of it to the center of man's own being, and the individual acceptance of God's ultimate accommodation in the Son. Encompassing this faith into himself, and encompassed by it, Adam cries out his great paean of praise, joy and triumph:

> O goodness infinite, goodness immense!
> That all this good of evil shall produce,
> And evil turn to good; more wonderful
> Than that which by creation first brought forth
> Light out of darkness. (XII, 469-73)

III. THE WORK OF THE SPIRIT

It is directly on the conclusion of this passage that we are introduced to the work of the Holy Spirit within the Christian individual and community. Milton uses the word "Comforter" (XII, 486), not in the modern flaccid and sentimental sense, but in the root meaning of strengthener, the fulfillment of the promise of the Father, "who shall dwell His Spirit within them" (XII, 487-88). The works of the Spirit are briefly but clearly set forth, the emphasis being upon freedom, faith, love, and understanding, without the slightest hint of a legalistic moralism. Written upon the heart of men, the "law" of faith works "through love . . . To guide them in all truth" (XII, 488-90). The result is an ethic of freedom, a morality of love, guided from within, and not forced from without. The work of the Holy Spirit is the subjective counterpart or complement of the objective fact of the Messiah, bringing about an inner transformation in response to that outward fact. George Hendry, in his enlightening discussion of the Holy Spirit, emphasizes the manner in which the freedom of the Christian man is preserved: "The grace of the Lord Jesus Christ does not override man's freedom; it respects it, it engages it to the full extent, it bows before it, because that is the only way in which a real relation, i.e., a personal relation, between God and man can be realized. Unless man's freedom is engaged, the only relation that could be established would be of the I-it order."[14]

[14] George S. Hendry, *The Holy Spirit in Christian Theology* (Philadelphia: Westminster Press, 1956), pp. 112-13.

The very respect for human integrity which characterizes God's dealings with men allows them to choose the grounds of their existence, and the very sin of Adam's usurpation upon deity is perennially repeated, so that, within the Church itself, men will turn "the sacred mysteries of heav'n To their own vile advantage" and treat as objects the very humanity which God refuses to treat as other than persons (XII, 509-10). Usurping now upon the Holy Spirit, churchly wolves will set up legalistic codes, "to themselves appropriating The Spirit of God, promis'd alike and giv'n To all believers" (XII, 518-20), as they seek to replace the free conscience under grace with external prescription under law and compulsion. In this way, the primary sin continues to express itself, to "force the Spirit of grace itself, and bind His consort liberty" (XII, 525-26). Man's self-assertive spirit eats away at the Church, and "unbuilds" God's "living temples" (XII, 526-27), which exist only as established in the Spirit of God and in the ministry of grace to man, not in the magistracy of power over man.

For those who do not repudiate the divine offer of reconciliation, the results are quite different. The frightened and frightening tactics of domination, the alternation between presumption and fear, the "swing to and fro between pride and anxiety" which, Barth says, characterizes the life of man, comes to an end in irrevocable acceptance of God, which is faith. "Faith is not an opinion replaceable by another opinion," Barth writes. "A temporary believer does not know what faith is. Faith means a final relationship."[15] Though the rela-

[15] *Outline*, p. 20.

tionship is final, it is not static, and we find in Adam
a marked growth from the time he kneels in penitent
petition after his fall, to the time he leaves the garden
"though sorrowing, yet in peace" (XI, 117). We have already noted the three alienations which fallen man suffers. When grace comes "unimplored, unsought" (III,
231) to Adam and Eve, they accept it—though, to be
sure, they are not aware of its full significance—and pray
for forgiveness. Here their choice is made, and growth
becomes possible. The Son, as mediator, interprets the
prayer for pardon as being in effect a prayer for the
restoration of relationship, for the reestablishment of
community (XI, 37-39). Following upon it, Adam is
once more in communion with God, while within himself "peace return'd" (XI, 153). He now accepts both
himself and Eve, whom he salutes with renewed joy and
confidence. The threefold reconciliation is implicit in
a speech which deserves full quotation. Adam says:

> Eve, easily may faith admit, that all
> The good which we enjoy, from heav'n descends;
> But that from us aught should ascend to heav'n
> So prevalent as to concern the mind
> Of God high-blest, or to incline his will,
> Hard to believe may seem; yet this will prayer,
> Or one short sigh of human breath, up-borne
> Ev'n to the seat of God. For since I sought
> By pray'r th' offended deity to appease,
> Kneel'd and before him humbl'd all my heart,
> Methought I saw him placable and mild,

Bending his ear; persuasion in me grew
That I was heard with favor; peace return'd
Home to my breast, and to my memory
His promise, that thy seed shall bruise our foe;
Which then not minded in dismay, yet now
Assures me that the bitterness of death
Is past, and we shall live. Whence, Hail to thee
Eve rightly call'd, mother of all mankind,
Mother of all things living, since by thee
Man is to live, and all things live for man.

    (XI, 141-161)

It is significant that the answer to Adam's prayer
comes through "persuasion in me" growing, and "peace
return'd," rather than through any external means or
explicit words (XI, 152-53). The answer to this prayer is
reorientation of life. After Adam's initial response in
faith, come a number of successive submissions to the
will of God, communicated by Michael, and Adam
grows in grace until he has attained to the paradise
within him upon which the epic closes. So it is that
Satan's conquest of man is abrogated.

IV. THE STRATEGY OF LIFE

As Satan had sought to pervert good into evil, life
into death, God has perverted the perversion itself, re-
versed its warp, and out of evil brought forth good. All
Satan's malice

. . . serv'd but to bring forth
Infinite goodness, grace and mercy shown
On man by him seduc't, but on himself

[85]

Treble confusion, wrath and vengeance pour'd.
  (i, 217-20)

By the Incarnation, Michael declares, the Son will crush Satan's strength over man, "defeating Sin and Death, his two main arms, And fix far deeper in his head their stings" (xii, 431-32). The Son's action will give "Death his death's wound" (iii, 252), that is, render him powerless over men who accept the accommodation of God to man's condition, the offer of divine acceptance. Death's "death wound" is delivered through man's assurance that a faithful death is "the gate of life" (xii, 571), for, in the face of that assurance, Death is powerless over man. The event is not haphazard or fortuitous, but a part of the nature of God, rooted in eternity in the divine will. Even before the fall of man, the Father and the Son had determined the utter destruction of all evil, the total erasure of sin, when the Son would ruin all his foes and with Death's "carcass glut the grave" (iii, 259). Even Sin knows it, and warns the rationalizing Satan and his deformed offspring, Death, that God's wrath "one day will destroy ye both" (ii, 734). The most dramatic statement of the fixed obliteration of evil comes from God the Father, who declares that he has drawn Death, Sin and their hell-hound children to earth

  to lick up the draff and filth
Which man's polluting sin with taint hath shed
On what was pure, till cramm'd and gorg'd, nigh burst
With suckt and glutted offal, at one sling
Of thy victorious arm, well-pleasing Son,
Both Sin and Death and yawning grave at last

Through Chaos hurl'd, obstruct the mouth of Hell
Forever, and seal up his ravenous jaws. (x, 630-37)

In those eight lines, Milton has, with masterful economy, achieved a dramatic image of the Last Judgment
totally devoid of the rather gruesome melodrama with
which Michaelangelo had treated the same subject.

The total shattering of all evil must come before man
can enter on the life everlasting. The Scriptures, as
Milton knew, and as modern theologians agree, do not
teach a doctrine of intrinsic human immortality, of the
self-sufficient continuity of human life. Mere unconditional immortality for man as man would mean not
heaven, but hell, for the unredeemed would continue
in a state of alienation from God, while the growth of
the redeemed towards God would be arrested and static.
Such immortality would be "a universe of death" (II,
622), which is the state of hell. It would be but "to
eternize woe" (XI, 60), and so God provides death as an
end to woe, denying intrinsic immortality to man, both
by banishing him from access to the Tree of Life (XI,
93-96) and by preventing Satan from using the fruit of
this tree like that of the first, "once more to delude"
(XI, 125). Death must complete the destruction of man's
sin, and then Death itself will be destroyed. The faithful man will find that death does not bring total obliteration, static continuity, or absorption into an Over-
soul and the loss of individuality in union with Brah-
man, after the teaching of the Indian religions. Against
each of these views the assurance of the resurrection of

a "spiritual" body is set as an unassailable block. The continuity is inescapably defined as personal. It is also communal. With the Final Judgment, in which the Son totally destroys evil, a new life is created, a life of full, but individual, community with God, with men, and with angels. The symbol for all this is not only the Son's dissolution of "Satan with his perverted world" (XII, 547), but even more, his raising

> From the conflagrant mass, purg'd and refin'd,
> New heav'ns, new earth, ages of endless date
> Founded in righteousness and peace and love,
> To bring forth fruits joy and eternal bliss.
> (XII, 548-551)

The vision of the new order, of the divine restructuring of existence into a new community, combines the personal and the corporate hope into one synoptic vision. Man's created purpose was not merely for community with God but with other men, as Milton's treatment of the Genesis saga clearly indicates, and so he cannot fully realize his destiny apart from human fellowship. The point, of central importance, indicates why the heavenly consummation comes jointly through individuality and society. Otherwise, man could not be man. Finally, it is clear that the conditions of everlasting life are provided by the act of God alone, so that the Christian view is of an immortality conferred by the act of God who calls it into being and provides for it the prerequisite "new heav'ns, new earth," without blotting out the individual personality of man. The result is Milton's picture of an existence totally dependent on the sole

absoluteness of God, which does not thereby deny the
personality of man by reabsorbing it, and of a personal
unending existence of the human being, which does not
thereby elevate man to the condition of independent
deity.

The heavenly life, then, consists in community, based
on individual personality, channeled through society,
and centered on God. Apart from God and the love of
God, the same constituents would produce hell, which,
in point of fact, is precisely what they did produce when
Satan and his legions sought heaven without God.

Against this background, the really significant death
of man comes at the point of his fall from God, rather
than at the point of physical mortality. Conversely, the
entrance into everlasting life comes at the point of
spiritual "rebirth," rather than at the point of physical
dissolution. The Kingdom of God is not limited to time
and place, but is "within," in the New Testament sense.
Eternal life becomes a possession for Adam within this
life, and although it is only partly realized here, it is
nonetheless present. This is the "paradise within thee,
happier far," with which Adam leaves the garden.
Adam's entry into this new life is indicated in connection with his prayer of penitence. His progress within
it is noted at various places, as we have seen, but is most
marked when his delight over God's perfect righteousness, goodness and love raises him entirely above despair
over his own sin. "O goodness infinite, goodness im-
mense," Adam cries out, as he fully recognizes the significance of Christ, and so is freed from the burdens which
he had borne upon his soul (xii, 469).

Entrance into the life everlasting is not, however, a repudiation of the life temporal. Rather, it is an affirmation of it, a dedication to it under the vocation of God. On the mount of vision, Adam has seen the continuous growth of evil in the world, has seen man's defiance of God, even to the supreme presumption of crucifying the Son. Under the impact of this total experience he turns, not away from the world, but toward it. There is neither an ignoring of the external things of the world, nor a denial of them, but rather a freedom from them. Albert Schweitzer writes that "the essence of Christianity is an affirmation of the world that has passed through a rejection of the world."[16] That sentence precisely summarizes what happens to Adam on the mount of vision. He returns from the angelic instruction with an understanding definable neither as optimism nor as pessimism. The best commentary on his new attitude may again be found in Schweitzer: "Christianity [cannot] definitely choose between pessimism and optimism. It is pessimistic, not only because, like Brahmanism and Buddhism, it realizes that imperfection, pain, and sorrow are essential features of the natural world, but for this additional and still more important reason, that in man it finds a will which does not answer to the will of the ethical God and which, therefore, is evil.

"Again, Christianity is optimistic, because it does not abandon this world, does not, as do Brahmanism and Buddhism, withdraw from it in negation of life and of the world, but assigns to man a place in this world and commands him to live in it and to work in it in the

[16] *Out of My Life and Thought,* p. 48.

spirit of the ethical God. Further, Christianity gives him the assurance that thereby God's purpose for the world and for man is being fulfilled."[17] Milton's epic thus closes on a union of sorrow and peace, of joy and sadness, in which sadness and sorrow, though present, are taken up into peace and joy. As transhistory, saga, and accommodation are complete, Adam and Eve, Everyman and Everywoman, leave the garden. When we see them next it will be as Christian and his wife Christiana, making the pilgrim's progress to the city of light. In valediction, Milton introduces them from transhistory into the life of the world:

> The world was all before them, where to choose
> Their place of rest, and Providence their guide:
> They hand in hand with wand'ring steps and slow,
> Through Eden took their solitary way.
> (XII, 646-49)

[17] *Christianity and the Religions of the World*, trans. Johanna Powers (London: George Allen and Unwin, 1923), pp. 75-76.

PART TWO

Pilgrim's Progress and the
Christian Life

5

THE WAY OF ALL PILGRIMS

MOVING FROM TRANSHISTORY INTO HISTORY, we find that the life of the archetypal man, Adam, gives way to the life of the archetypal Christian. The full vision of Christianity, presented in *Paradise Lost* through symbol and accommodation, sets the stage for all human thought and experience. The movement in Milton's epic is from divine reality to human situation, and the method is the accommodation, by vital symbols, of transcendent truth to human understanding. In *The Pilgrim's Progress,* the vision is implemented in the way, the faith caught up in works, and the movement is from the city of man to the city of God. The method of allegory in Bunyan's work is broad, so that all Christian life is set forth in, and explained by, the lives of his pilgrims. Milton carries us from the heavenly city to the earthly situation, and Bunyan reverses the course, taking us "from this world to that which is to come." Between the two works, the cycle is completed and the union of faith and life made explicit.

I. DEPARTURE AND MOTIVES

Pilgrim's Progress opens with the vision of a man clothed in rags, symbolic of the ultimate poverty of humanity, and weighed down by the burden of guilt which he carries on his back. His first words are, "What shall I do?" (9) Knowing only the misery of man's condition, he finds no way of escape; he sees only part of the vision—man's evil—and from this he seeks release. As his understanding deepens, he adds three significant words to his earlier question: "What shall I do *to be saved?*" (10) By these words, Bunyan indicates his protagonist's comprehension of the necessary distinction between escape and rescue, a distinction we have already treated (Part I, Chap. 4). Knowing his sin, and his inability to escape unaided, without entering into even greater sin, the pilgrim is now prepared for the meeting with Evangelist, who points to the way of Christ and directs the pilgrim to the Wicket Gate.

The Gate by which the pilgrim enters upon the way is Christ, according to the symbolism by which Jesus had declared, "I am the door."[1] This identification of Christ with the Gate is explicit in Part II ("the Gate which is Christ") of *The Pilgrim's Progress* (197-204), but is clearly implicit here, so that the Christian begins with the incarnation and moves on toward God. Men tend to assume they can know God as he is, often judging Christ by his conformity to a prior human image of God. Christianity, however, denies that finite and sinful creatures can know God, with any great clarity, apart from Christ. Bunyan thus indicates that the pilgrim knows virtually nothing of God until he enters the Gate which God has provided, and that henceforth, his knowledge increases as he advances along the route of pilgrimage.

Pilgrim's Progress consists of two parts, each complete

[1] John 10:1-18, *passim.*

in itself. The first recounts the full journey of the pilgrim, who was called Graceless and is now known as Christian, from the City of Destruction to the Celestial City. Concerned as it is with the individual, this first part presents one facet of the Christian life, and does not deal primarily with the larger life of the Christian community. The second part of the allegory supplies the perspective of the church, the body of Christians moving over the same ground that Christian had earlier covered. At first there is Christian's wife, Christiana, who had abandoned him to his journey alone, but who now sets out to follow him with their four sons and a charming young girl named Mercy. Others are added to this group as the pilgrimage proceeds, and finally there is a large company of diverse members who complete the journey together. By the device of two juxtaposed narratives, Bunyan provides a stereoscopic view of the Christian life, fully three-dimensional and vital in its perspectives, expressing both the individual and the corporate aspects of the pilgrimage.

From the total number of the pilgrims in both parts of the allegory, we see the various types of Christian life and the problems, temptations, and joys incident to each. Not all the pilgrims set out for the same reason, and each has a somewhat different experience of the way. Christian leaves the City of Destruction because of a compelling sense of doom, and a sort of numinous fear, so that he sets out with less sense of his goal than of his need. Christiana, on the other hand, begins her journey in response to a specific invitation from the King of Heaven, and with a clear sense both of favorable destiny and of destination. Further, it is at the invitation of Christiana, rather than of God, that young Mercy begins her pilgrimage, while Hopeful joins Christian on his lonely way after the martyrdom of Christian's earlier companion, Faithful. Others leave for equally appropriate and personal reasons, but all go through the same Gate, and over the same way. As Augustine put it, "Christ as God is the fatherland where we are going; Christ as man is the way by which we go."[2] The way is the same, but the wayfarers differ and, therefore, so does the wayfaring. Each learns for himself and in terms of his own character "how to act faith" (213), to use the words of Christiana, and each increases in the love for God and for God's people, which is the only ultimately satisfactory motive for acting the Christian faith.

The pilgrims who complete the journey from destruction to fulfillment do so out of "the love that they bear to the King of this place" (172), and they continue in the way only because, like Christian, they prefer the person, company, and servants of Christ over the enticements of Apollyon (61-62). No other motivation is ultimately sufficient to sustain the pilgrims in the completion of so difficult a way. Each who perseveres does so in order that, as young Samuel puts it, "I may see God, and serve him without weariness; that I may see Christ and love him everlastingly; that I may have that fulness of the Holy Spirit in me, that I can by no means here enjoy" (238). Heaven is sought not because it is "a palace and state most blessed," but because God is the center

[2] *Sermons*, 124.3.

of heaven, and it is only for that reason that heaven is the palace and state most blessed (238).

The love of God, then, is clearly central. Without it, man's alienation cannot be overcome, or his fulfillment attained. We have developed in some detail, in Chapter 3, the threefold alienation from which Adam suffers, as his sin sets him at odds with God, with his neighbor, and with himself. This isolation of the self is overcome, as we have seen, only by reconciliation with God, and this reconciliation comes in its turn only through the action of God himself, in and through Christ. In Christ, God acts so that his justice and mercy, his power and his love, are at one, and it is only through such divine action that man can be rescued from imprisonment to his own self-critical or self-satisfied self. No merely human efforts will suffice, for, as Hopeful says of himself, man commits enough sin in one duty to seal his own isolation; Augustine says, our greatest virtues are but splendid vices (149). Man, then, must enter through the one Gate.

Along the way, there are a number of pseudo-pilgrims who have entered over the wall rather than through the Gate, and they contend that their entry is effective enough, since it has put them on the road in a manner best suited to their own conditions; it is, in other words, more convenient for them. Of the convenient, Kierkegaard writes that it should be applied "wherever it can be applied, in relation to everything which is in such a sense a thing that this thing can be possessed irrespective of the way in which it is possessed, so that one can have it either in this way or the other; for when such

[99]

is the case, the convenient and comfortable way is undeniably to be preferred." Such a "convenient and comfortable" view of the way is held by those who enter it apart from the Gate, and who never complete the journey. Kierkegaard aptly continues: "But the eternal is not a thing which can be had regardless of the way in which it is acquired; no, the eternal is not really a thing, but is the way in which it is acquired. The eternal is acquired in *one* way, and the eternal is different from everything else precisely for the fact that it can be acquired only in a single way."[3] Eternal life, then, *is* "the way in which it is acquired," and that way is the Christ-Gate, which provides the only ultimate means of reconciliation.

This reconciliation, though primarily with God, is also with other selves and with the individual self. Once the self is properly related to its creator, it is ready for a proper relation with other creatures and with itself as a part of creation. These relations are expressions of love, which Augustine defines as "a motion of the soul whose purpose is to enjoy God for his own sake, and ourselves and our neighbor for the sake of God."[4]

Contradicting the operation of this love, it is one function of the demonic agents along the route of the pilgrims to set up "a difference between a man and himself" (317), to make man be "unmerciful to himself," to dwell with ruin (215, 218), and to love his ease and comfort more than he loves himself (228). The demonic

[3] Soren Kierkegaard, *Attack upon Christendom*, trans. Walter Lowrie (Princeton: Princeton University Press, 1944), p. 100.
[4] *Christian Doctrine*, 3. 10. 16.

plays on a self-love which is really a form of self-hate, and seeks to develop a destruction of the self which is consequent on an unhealthy affirmation of the self. On the other hand, a healthy and proper self-love is possible only as corollary to the love of God, issuing in what Milton in *Paradise Lost* called "self-esteem, grounded on just and right Well manag'd" (VIII, 572-73). It is in this sense that Mercy "yearned over her own soul," fell "in love with her own salvation" and followed Christiana "to seek to live forever" (194, 197, 205). In Augustine's words, "it is impossible for one who loves God not to love himself."[5] The love of God above and beyond the self so alters the face of life that it becomes possible to love both neighbor and self, and to seek in heaven the consummation of charity in companionship with immortals (193).

What may have begun in fear, as with Christian, must give place to this determinative love, if it is to attain to the completion of the way. But although fear may tend to set the pilgrim on his way, as Christian clearly feels that it does (160), fear as such is not necessarily a virtue, and may be a serious form of sin. It may be the fear of difficulty which prevents false pilgrims from completing the journey, or it may be the fear of public opinion, what Hopeful called the "fear of men" (162), that makes man conform to the contemporary norms of society rather than to the eternal norm of Christ. To such temptations all the pilgrims are subjected, some

[5] Waldo Beach and H. Richard Niebuhr, eds., *Christian Ethics, Sources of the Living Tradition* (New York: The Ronald Press, 1955), p. 117.

succumbing to them. Worst of all, perhaps, is the fear of punishment, the "fear of the torments of hell" which Hopeful says makes some men temporarily "hot for heaven" (162). The difficulty here, as Christian points out, is that "the fear of the halter" may exist apart from any "detestation of the offense" which leads to the halter (163). Men so affected "seem hot for heaven so long as the flames of hell are about their ears, yet when that terror is a little over, they betake themselves to second thoughts" (162). "From those who fear punishment," Augustine said, "grace is hidden."[6]

But there is another type of fear to which Augustine referred when he wrote that "piety begins with fear and is perfected in love."[7] This is the productive fear which Christian experienced so often in the earlier stages of his journey, and which was one part of his incentive for leaving the City of Destruction. Not all the pilgrims set out from a fear of the consequences of sin, and some experience virtually no sense of fear in the ordinary ways, but for Christian himself, fear is one motive for seeking God. In his experience, as in that of Kierkegaard, it was necessary to have feared God before he could come to love him. Christian's course may be marked in terms of Alfred North Whitehead's three stages in the development of religion: "It is the transition from God the void [before the allegory opens] to God the enemy [the stage of frustrated fear with which the story begins], and from God the enemy to God the

[6] *Basic Writings*, Vol. 1, p. 503.
[7] *Earlier Writings*, p. 240.

companion, [beginning when Christian enters the Gate]."[8]

None of these fears is merely the common form of reflex or adrenal fear which all men experience, in varying degrees, when faced with impinging danger. Adrenal fear and alarm is common enough in Bunyan's story, but it is not determinative for the true pilgrims, and is always driven out either by a larger and nobler fear or by impetus from the love to which that fear is akin. This noblest fear is the pilgrim's fear of offending against the love of God, and it tends in its turn to "take away from them their pitiful old self-holiness" (161). The thing that is dreaded is not punishment, but separation from God, whether because of active evil or passive self-righteousness. Fear grounded in guilt is not enough, though it may be a beginning. What is necessary is an entire and radical reorientation and redirection of life. "When your heart is thus established in Christ," Luther wrote, "you are an enemy of sin out of love and not out of fear of punishment."[9]

One further form of fear afflicts Christian, both as he attempts to cross over the Slough of Despond on his way to the Wicket Gate, and as he crosses the final River of Death to the celestial country. This fear is a form of deficient faith, an inadequate reliance on the grace of God which may afflict even the redeemed. It is a final mark of continuing faithlessness, even in the faithful,

[8] Alfred North Whitehead, *Religion in the Making* (Cambridge: Cambridge University Press, 1927), p. 6.

[9] Martin Luther, *A Compend of Luther's Theology*, ed. Hugh Thompson Kerr, Jr. (Philadelphia: Westminster Press, 1943), p. 55.

so that, at the very outset of his pilgrimage, Christian is driven into the Slough of Despond by fear which "followed me so hard" (16), and again, at the end of his course, he almost goes under the waters of the river out of "horror of mind and hearty fears that he should die in that river and never obtain entrance" to the heavenly city (167). In each instance, Christian is afflicted by a deeply morbid sense of sin, the retention of which is, in itself, a form of sin even in the Christian whose life has been radically reoriented toward God.

The righteousness of the Christian is never a mere sinlessness, relieved from all blemishes. It is not a thing pure and apart, but is a center of confidence, a direction of aspiration, a basic character of charity, lived within the framework of common liabilities. All Bunyan's pilgrims continue to sin in greater and lesser degrees, and are not to be distinguished from others by the flawlessness of their lives, as much as by the center of their patriotism. The true pilgrims clearly place their loyalties in the heavenly city, and, despite occasional errings, move in general in that direction. It is this patriotism and loyalty which makes them appear as fools to the citizens of the present world. The criticisms most commonly applied to them are that they are fools and unmanly, not normally human.

The criteria for wisdom and for humanity are under continuous dispute, at least by implication, throughout *Pilgrim's Progress*. Obstinate tells the wayfaring Christian to "be wise" (13), Vanity Fair calls him a madman (96), and his wife thinks him neurotic (189). In the second part of the allegory, when Christiana sets out to follow her husband, she is called a fool and insane, while Obstinate and Pliable are held up as models of wisdom (193-96). On the question of humanity, Worldly-wise-man warns Christian that the Bible can "unman men" (20), and Shame tells Faithful that his conscience is "unmanly" (77). From the Christian point of view, it is held that those who leave the way to the heavenly city to delve in Demas' silver mine will never be "their own men again" (113), and Christian is said to have "played the man" in opposing Apollyon (253).

The divergence apparent in these instances, as in many others, is again traceable to the matter of rooted loyalties. For each of the true pilgrims, loyalty is centered in God, and the norm both of manhood and wisdom is discovered in Christ. The ultimate criterion of life is found to reside neither in transience, as with the City of Destruction, nor in human legalism, as with the Village of Morality, nor in popular materialism, as in Vanity Fair, but only in the normative person of Christ. For this reason, the Christians must enter through the Wicket Gate, and so their basic judgments of wisdom and of humanity differ radically from those of all others they meet. The regnant God in the celestial city is the goal of the pilgrim's way, the incarnate Son on earth is the norm of the pilgrim's life and thought. Without the Son there would be no true knowledge of the entry and the way to the Father, so that all who would attain everlasting communion with God must begin by coming in at the Gate. That is an inescapable absolute of the pilgrimage.

II. THE TWO RELATIVISMS

Along with this absolute there is much relativism among the pilgrims. Indeed, relativism is as much found among the true pilgrims as among the false, though the character of one group's relativism differs entirely from that of the other. For the Christian pilgrims, there are marked and highly relative differences of response to the way, but there is also commitment to the way itself. For the pseudo-pilgrims, relativism appears in their various ways of entry and advance, one way being judged as valid as another. After scaling the wall, Formalist and Hypocrisy ask: "If we get into the way, what matter which way we get in? If we are in, we are in" (43). Similarly, they get out of the way when they come to the Hill Difficulty, and choose the seemingly easier paths marked Danger and Destruction. One route being as good as another, they naturally choose those which appear the more convenient. Later, Christian meets two men who have turned back from the way because of the horrors of the Valley of the Shadow of Death. When Christian persists in going forward along the dangerous road which they have just abandoned, they comment: "Be it thy way, we will not choose it for ours" (66). Other similar examples of secular relativism might be cited, but these are sufficient: the way is seen as relative to man, determined by man. Viewing the landscape of reality from the perspective of the self, all falls into place in terms of convenience and acceptability to the individual. In this manner the primary sin asserts itself again: man is god, the *I* is god, and his own knowledge of good and evil is determinative. The entrance, the way, and even the goal, are relative to the individuals who judge. Thus Ignorance says to Hopeful and Christian: "Be content to follow the religion of your country, and I will follow the religion of mine. I hope all will be well" (132).

In all this, the Christian assumptions are not attacked so much as repudiated by the false pilgrims. Without a recognition of the primary sin of self-deification, they cannot see the dangers involved in making pilgrimage only to please themselves. Their relativism is that of the absolute self, by which all else is judged.

The Christian pilgrims' relativism, on the other hand, is that of the relative self before an absolute God. The way established by God can neither be short cut, nor made over, nor avoided, but experience of the one way will vary greatly according to the individual temper of the wayfarers. In this regard, the experience of various pilgrims may be compared to that of Christian, who is clearly the most prideful of those who eventually reach the heavenly city. It is due to his pride, and his inability to meet, on his own terms, the proud standards which he holds up for himself, that Christian falls into the Slough of Despond, which all others among the faithful pass without mishap. So, too, the Valley of Humiliation is a dreadful place for Christian, while of this valley the other pilgrims are told that "here is nothing to hurt us unless we procure it to ourselves" (249). Mercy and her companions of part two find it a delightful place, and Mr. Great-heart declares that "though Christian had the hard hap to meet here with Apollyon and to enter with him a brisk encounter, yet I must tell you, that in former times men have met with angels here, have found pearls here, and have in this place found the words of life" (251). Similarly with the Valley of the Shadow of Death: whereas Christian found it a place of horrors, to Faithful it was a sunshine place (80) and it was never quieter than when Mr. Fearing passed through it (265). Of all the pilgrims, Christian, because of his pride, is the least able to pass in peace through the valleys of Humiliation and of the Shadow of Death.

Faithful is a more fleshly man than Christian, less profound perhaps, and certainly less proud. His temptations accordingly differ from Christian's, and as he is less morbidly fearful about his own guilt, he has no difficulty at the Slough of Despond. He does, however, have a tempting encounter with the lustful Madam Wanton outside the Gate, and she promises him "all manner of content." He is so strongly attracted to her that, as he says, "I know not whether I did wholly escape her or no" (73). More humble than Christian, but also more conventional, he is tempted in the Valley of Humiliation not by the massive onslaughts of Apollyon but by the rather bourgeois appeals of Discontent and Shame, who taunt him with his violation of conventional mores (76-8).

Other individual differences make for varied experiences of the way. Mr. Fearing, utterly unconcerned with outward dangers, has "a Slough of Despond in his mind, a Slough that he carried everywhere with him, or else he could never have been as he was" (263). Mr. Feeble-mind is "carried up" the Hill Difficulty over which all the other pilgrims toil (281), and the shepherds in the Delectable Mountains call on each of the weaker pilgrims by name, as they would otherwise be "most subject to draw back" (299). Each of the principal pilgrims sets out in a fashion somewhat different from that of the others, Christian with a deep, numinous awe, Christiana with middle class directness, the children because they are told to go, and Valiant-for-truth with the forthrightness of the young knight-errant: "I believed and therefore came out, got into the way, fought all that set themselves against me, and by believing am come to this place" (309).

For all of the true pilgrims, though, "the way is the way, and there's an end" (250). They may temporarily persuade themselves, as Christian does, that there is a better path, but always they return to the way itself, to endure there whatever their own failures may procure to themselves until they complete the entrance of the Wicket Gate by entrance into the Celestial Gate. The movement is from earthly disclosure through Christ to heavenly culmination with God. The Kingdom of Heaven must thus be entered through the two gates, the one at the beginning and the other at the end. Between the two is the inescapable road of pilgrimage. To it, Christian is directed at the Wicket Gate: "Look before thee: dost thou see this narrow way? *That* is the way thou must go. It was cast up by the patriarchs, prophets, Christ, and his apostles, and it is as straight as a rule can make it. This is the way thou must go" (29).

As Reinhold Niebuhr puts it, "The Kingdom of Heaven as it *has come* in Christ means a disclosure of the meaning of history but not the full realization of that meaning. That is anticipated in the Kingdom which *is to come*, that is, in the culmination of history. . . . Thus history as we know it is regarded as an 'interim' between the disclosure and the fulfillment of its meaning."[10] The Christian accepts the inescapable absoluteness of the disclosure and of the fulfillment, as both are wholly determined by the will of God, and accepts the relativities of the "interim" through which he passes from the one to the other.

III. THE SLOW ADVANCE

Entrance at the Wicket Gate can establish a final commitment to God, but it does not and cannot establish a static relationship. Entrance provides the possibility of growth, and growth precludes a static condition. Thus the naive hope of Mercy is disappointed, and she discovers that by entering upon the way she has not left danger and sorrow behind (208), as she had expected. An apt description of the difficult life of Christian wayfaring comes from Old Honest, who says: "Sometimes our way is clean, sometimes foul: sometimes up hill, sometimes down hill. We are seldom at a certainty" (289).

In this condition, beset by repeated difficulties within and without, "seldom at a certainty," the pilgrims "keep by the pole, and do by compass steer from sin to grace" (298). Holding to their goal of communion with God,

[10] Niebuhr, *The Nature and Destiny of Man, A Christian Interpretation* (New York: Charles Scribner's Sons, 1949), Vol. II, p. 288.

they nonetheless do not have the goal always before their
eyes, and they move slowly. When Evangelist first directs
Christian, it is not for the full journey, and he gives
him as his goal not the City of Zion, but the Wicket
Gate and the light which he dimly sees shining about
it. When Pliable briefly joins Christian, he asks him if
he knows the whole way to the "desired place," and
Christian replies that he has only been directed "to a
little Gate that is before us, where we shall receive in-
structions about the way" (13). So it is again in the
second part of the allegory that when one of the children
asks the guide, Mr. Great-heart, whether they can see
to the end, he is merely told to "look to your feet, for
you shall presently be among the snares" (256). The pilgrimage is long, and must be taken one step at a time.
"Come, let us venture," says Mercy at the Slough of
Despond, "only let us be wary" (198).

The way is always venturesome, and the pilgrim is
sometimes not wary. Christian falls into the Slough of
Despond, and Pliable deserts him to return to the City
of Destruction. Released from the Slough, Christian
again takes up his way toward the Gate, but is diverted
by Mr. Worldly-wiseman, who persuades him to work
out his own deliverance by improving his character, and
so Christian sets out for the Village of Morality, to profit
from the counsel of Mr. Legality. On the way, however,
he becomes afraid that Mount Sinai will avalanche down
upon him and so he turns from legalism, and is once
more encountered by Evangelist who again directs him
to the Wicket Gate. Once entered there, he is directed
to the House of the Interpreter, who further instructs

him, and sends him on for the next part of his journey. All this while he has been carrying upon his back the great weight of his guilt, and he is relieved of this burden only when he comes to the cross standing above an empty tomb. Beyond this point he is joined by Formalist and Hypocrisy, who soon apostatize, so that he climbs the Hill Difficulty alone and arrives at the House Beautiful on its summit, where he is refreshed and given further instruction. He next descends into the Valley of Humiliation, and passes on through the Valley of the Shadow of Death, after which he joins Faithful for his first Christian companionship on the road. In Vanity Fair, Faithful is martyred, but his example is such that Hopeful now joins Christian on the way. Together they withstand the blandishments of Demas to turn aside to his silvermine, but they themselves shortly seek an easier path by crossing over into By-Path Meadow, and so are imprisoned by Giant Despair in Doubting Castle. Escaping after a harrowing period in the castle dungeon, they make their way to the Delectable Mountains where they are entertained, instructed and refreshed by the shepherds of Emmanuel's Land. They next meet with Ignorance on the way, pass through their final hazard in the Enchanted Ground, and enter Beulah Land, where they are royally welcomed. Finally, they cross the River of Death and are received with great rejoicing into the City of God. The movement is clearly a matter of gradual stages. From House Beautiful, the pilgrim can see only to the Delectable Mountains, from the Delectable Mountains, he can see the glory and the gate of heaven, and from Beulah, he sees the heavenly city itself. The growth of vision is as gradual as is advance along the way, and throughout, the pilgrims must "look to their feet" (256). As God the Father says in *Paradise Lost,*

Light after light well us'd they shall attain,
And to the end persisting, safe arrive. (III, 196-97)

6

GOOD AND EVIL

SAFE ARRIVAL at the goal is no simple matter. There are demons to be met and giants, the animosity of cities and things which "cared not for Christian's sword" (67). There are valleys and mountains and pits and grounds from which enchantment rises like the miasmatic mist. But first and foremost are the temptations of apparent moral goodness, for things are never as simple as they seem.

I. THE DECEIT OF MORALISM

The pilgrim Christian is a man of intense moral sensitivity. He begins his journey with a burden of conscientious scruples on his back such as none of the other pilgrims ever appear to bear. Weighed down by this burden, and driven on by moral fears, he falls into the Slough of Despond. The preoccupation with good and evil, with moral slavery and moral deliverance, which impelled him to set out for the Wicket Gate, has produced in him anxiety, unrelieved by faith, a state clearly symbolized by his wallowing in the mire of despond.

Once Christian has been released from the Slough of Despond, however, his moral preoccupation at once betrays him into another danger. We have already discussed, in connection with *Paradise Lost*, Karl Barth's view of man's natural fluctuation between anxiety and pride, and we now see the same principles at work in *Pilgrim's Progress*, as Christian leaves the way to seek satisfaction in the Village of Morality under the tutelage of a gentleman named Legality, and his son, Civility. Here, as elsewhere in Bunyan, the names are eloquent in their simplicity. Christian's notion is that he can, in the perennially applicable terms, "be good," "do right," and thus improve his character until the burden no longer troubles him. To this end he is urged by Mr. Worldly-wiseman to seek release in Morality, but as he approaches the village he becomes increasingly concerned with the ominous appearance of the mountain of the law, Sinai, which seems to offer impinging threats of avalanche, and so of imposing even greater burdens upon him. In fear, Christian turns back toward the way he had abandoned.

Now the Village of Morality cannot be regarded, by normal civilized standards, as an evil place. It is, indeed, a seat of virtue, and Mr. Worldly-wiseman who directs Christian there is a "gentleman," a man of obvious "wisdom," a conspicuous pillar of his community, and, as Bunyan makes clear, a church-goer (22-24). His advice to Christian is "good" advice, and he protests that Christian must not return to the evil City of Destruction from whence he came, but that he should rather go on to live honestly among honest neighbors. The road which he directs him to take is a "high" road. Although Mr. Worldly-wiseman can in no sense be regarded as a fool, a débauché or a shyster, he is nonetheless a charlatan, who offers a quack remedy for a real malady. His morality is the product of pride, and for that reason is inherently sinful, though superficially good. What Christian needs, and eventually finds, is not a new code of action but a new ordering of life. When the new ordering of life comes, it is followed by a new morality, but before it comes, morality is but a bypass from the way of fulfillment.

We have seen that the fall of Adam and Eve was in one sense a fall to virtue, for they became arbiters of good and evil. In the same sense the high road to the Village of Morality is a road to ruin. Reinhold Niebuhr writes that "moral pride is the pretension of finite man that his highly conditioned virtue is the final righteousness and that his very relative moral standards are absolute. Moral pride thus makes virtue the very vehicle of sin, a fact which explains why the New Testament is so critical of the righteous in comparison with 'publicans and sinners.' This note in the Bible distinguishes Biblical moral theory from all simple moralism, including Christian moralism."[1] Such moralism, Evangelist tells Christian as he redirects him to the Wicket Gate, "is not able to set thee free from thy burden" (25).

But moralism as a delusion is found not only outside the Wicket Gate, but beyond it, as well. Indeed, the moralist can make his way over the wall onto the route of the pilgrims (although he cannot enter by the Gate because, as a moralist, he refuses to admit any need for what is symbolized by the Gate), and he can make his way up to the final goal, to the Celestial City itself. But having come so far, the moralist finds that he is at the last thrust into the bypass to hell which is located under

[1] *The Nature and Destiny of Man*, Vol. I, p. 199.

the very shadow of heaven, for, as Bunyan says, "I saw that there was a way to hell, even from the gates of heaven, as well as from the City of Destruction" (173). No symbols can more clearly indicate the relation of mere morality to godliness: so near, and yet so infinitely far removed.

The moralist, who at the end is thrust into the bypass to hell where he had expected to enter heaven, is called Ignorance, and he is a charming figure. We like him instinctively, perhaps because he is so close to the ideal of our culture. Living "as other good people do" (131) by standards which seem self-evident in his own country, true to the "inner" voice of his conscience, quietly and pleasantly content with his heart's virtue, he says that "I am always full of good motions, that come into my mind to comfort me as I walk" (153-54). According to every outward standard of our own middle class society, Ignorance is a good man, a charming companion, and a stout pillar of virtue. He staunchly repudiates what he thinks might "loosen the reins of our lust, and tolerate us to live as we list" (157); he is not seduced into the net of the black demonic flatterer who tricks Hopeful and Christian by his white robes and specious appeal; neither, again, does the Enchanted Ground seem to prove such a trial to Ignorance as it does to the two true pilgrims. He follows the even tenor of his way without any conspicuous sin, and with virtues which are both apparent and appealing. But—the objection is both central and determinative—he refuses to acknowledge that he is himself not good, but a sinner. "I will never believe," he declares, "that my heart is thus bad" (155).

He focuses on good actions rather than on the need for redemption at the core of his personality, and although he is attractive, he is not regenerate. His end is, therefore, the bypass to hell, for he has failed to see the truth of Hopeful's realistic confession for himself, that "I have committed sin enough in one duty to send me to hell." He is aptly called Ignorance, for he is ignorant of himself. "In other living creatures," Boethius writes, "the ignorance of themselves is nature; but in men it is vice."[2]

Ignorance stands as the perennial "peace of mind" man, intent on the power of positive thinking, totally unwilling to face criticism of his own self-assertion disguised as religion. Not that he is pompous, for Bunyan is too realistic an observer and too subtle an allegorist to allow us to dismiss Ignorance for social faults. Ignorance, as a proponent of "positive thinking," is a winning figure. He is a "brisk lad," who has always been a good liver, a consistent tither, and who enters the pilgrim's way over the wall from "a fine pleasant green lane that comes down" from the Country of Conceit (132). Immensely engaging, he has the unaffected self-confidence of the man whose heart tells him that he is good and all is well. Accentuating the power of such positive thinking, he repudiates the efforts of Christian and Hopeful to show him the negation which man bears at the core of his being. "Luther rightly insisted," Reinhold Niebuhr writes, "that the unwillingness of the sinner to be regarded as a sinner was the final form of sin. The final proof that man no longer knows God is

[2] Boethius, *The Consolations of Philosophy*, ed. H. F. Stewart (New York: G. P. Putnam's Sons, 1918), Vol. II, v.88-89, 2:5.

that he does not know his own sin."[3] Had Ignorance known the norm by which all humanity is gauged, he would not have accepted his heart's glow in lieu of necessary righteousness; but he did not know the norm, and neither Christian nor Hopeful could show it to him. In the words of Francis de Sales, "there is a difference between possessing the presence of God and having the 'feeling' of his presence."[4] Ignorance is ignorant of that difference.

II. THE SECULAR IDOLATRY

If morality may became a delusion, so may society become a false god, as indeed it does in Vanity Fair. At the very outset of the Vanity Fair passages, Bunyan tells us that the Fair was established by Beelzebub and his cohorts to ensnare pilgrims, and he reminds us throughout the episode that this entire region is a province of the devil's activity and control. This, then, is so obviously a "bad" place that we are likely to dismiss it as such without looking more deeply into Bunyan's allegory for its significance and its values.

Actually, Vanity Fair is not an altogether undesirable place, when judged by the standards of modern civilization. It is an active market town, whose trade is lively and varied. It has its laws and religion, and it vigorously prosecutes all who do not live up to these. When Christian and Faithful enter this bustling and business-like

---

[3] *The Nature and Destiny of Man*, Vol. I, p. 200.
[4] Francis de Sales, *Spiritual Conferences*, trans. Abbot Gasquet and Canon Mackey (Westminster, Maryland: The Newman Bookshop, 1943), pp. 157-58.

town, they are at once marked down as non-conformists, and later as active subverters of the town's most cherished values. Faithful is brought to trial and before judge and jury is condemned as a traitor and a heretic. It is significant that these two convictions are linked together, for, in this way, Bunyan underscores the type of purely relative and sociologically conditioned values which are enshrined in his allegorical city of this world.

At the trial, three witnesses appear against Faithful, and only one of these even mentions the name of the Fair's prince, Beelzebub, against whom Faithful has "traitorously" spoken. The other two witnesses, who are the first to appear, speak of Faithful's general disloyalty to law and his religious divergence. Surely such accusations represent an apparently solid and high-minded interest in saving the community from corruption, and in preserving its highest values. The first witness is much aggrieved that Faithful has referred to Vanity Fair as an un-Christian community, while the second is similarly disturbed that Faithful had said that "our religion was naught, and such by which a man could by no means please God . . . that we still do worship in vain, are yet in our sins, and finally shall be damned." Thus, it is charged, did Faithful "not only condemn all our laudable doings, but us in the doing of them" (100). These are not the allegations of an irreligious community, however demonic its loyalties may be, and that is precisely the point. It is Beelzebub's strategy to make Vanity Fair a religious society, even a society in which citizens resent being faced with the fact that they are not Christian. Of the three witnesses against Faithful as a "runagate, heretic and traitor," only the last honestly mentions and honors the name of "our noble Prince Beelzebub," and this witness is named Pickthank (101). It is almost as though he wanted to reassure the demon, who had so consistently interested himself in the well-being of Vanity Fair, that he still had loyal servants, whatever the religious professions might be.

That the first two witnesses have such religious concerns, and especially that they do not once mention Beelzebub, are strong marks of the demonic success. "The more he prevails in our lives," Denis de Rougemont writes in his brilliant contemporary study of the devil, "the less we are able to recognize him. The more effective he is, the less dangerous he appears. His own activity conceals him from the eyes of the one it dominates. He vanishes in his success, and his triumph is his incognito."[5]

The triumph is surely there. Although Vanity Fair has prosperity, comfort, law, and religion, it gives not the slightest sign of ever having encouraged love. Its society is bound together by mutual interests and mutual antagonisms, by tradition, envy, and superstition, but in no sense by charity. Literally everything is for sale. It is what Walter Rauschenbusch meant by "the kingdom of evil": "Beyond the feeble and short-lived individual towers the social group as a super-personal entity, dominating the individual, assimilating him to its moral standards, and enforcing them by the social sanctions of approval or disapproval."[6]

[5] De Rougemont, *op.cit.*, p. 46.
[6] Beach and Niebuhr, *op.cit.*, pp. 464-65.

Idealizing its own interests and concerns, Vanity Fair achieves the apotheosis of the law of averages, the idolatry of conformity to the culturally relative, but culturally established, norms of a particular society. Its religion exalts the partial to a pseudo-universal status, and claims finality for the contingent. Faced with such pretension, Faithful had to make a commitment, and so "set himself against that which had set itself against him that is higher than the highest" (99). Having achieved the most patent goals of "success," Vanity Fair regards its own standards as self-justifying, and identifies its enemies with the enemies of religion. So, to quote again from De Rougemont, "the devil prevents us from recognizing God in Jesus Christ, but inversely he prevents us also from recognizing ourselves in our idols."[7]

In this instance the idol is the society, which assumes deity to itself in demanding the individual's unconditioned loyalty, and in maintaining that its own pretensions are the final criteria for the life of the individual. As one following in the way "cast up by . . . prophets," Faithful must deny such a pretension. For his denial he is martyred, and martyred by men who passionately believe that as a heretic-traitor he does not deserve to live longer. In the words of Pascal, "men never do evil so completely and cheerfully as when they do it from religious conviction."[8] Bunyan gives even the devil his due.

Although martyrdom is not required of Christian, he adopts the same attitude toward Vanity Fair as does

[7] De Rougemont, *op.cit.*, p. 119.
[8] Pascal, *op.cit.*, No. 894, p. 314.

Faithful, that of quiet protest and passive suffering. Neither complains, and neither rails. Even though the pain which they endure together is unjustly inflicted, they treat it as an issue to be met, not as a problem to be solved. Confronted with such an attitude, Vanity Fair must either change its own standards or destroy Faithful, and, within the development of *Pilgrim's Progress*, it changes only after destroying Faithful.

This passive protest represents one of the two attitudes taken by Christians toward Vanity Fair and its evils. The second attitude is that adopted by the party of pilgrims in the second part of the allegory. When Christiana and her companions, under the guidance of Mr. Great-heart, arrive at Vanity Fair, they find a changed atmosphere, "more moderate now than formerly." True Christians are more in evidence, and conditions in general have improved, for "the blood of Faithful lieth with load upon them till now, for since they burned him, they have been ashamed to burn any more" (289). The town, however, is now afflicted by a "monster out of the woods" who "slew many of the people" and would "carry away their children" (291). Whereas, in the earlier narrative, reformation of evil could be stimulated only by martyrdom, it is clear that martyrdom before the monster would be useless waste. Its threat upon individual lives can only be checked by vigorous resistance, and so the Christian community conducts an attack upon the marauder, cripples it, and gives protection to all the citizens of the town. Bunyan indicates that both passive suffering and overt assault upon evil, as circumstances may require, are appropriate for the Christian who makes his way through this world to the celestial city.

III. THE DEMONS AND THE GIANTS

The monster who comes out of the woods to slay the people of Vanity Fair and to take away their children is said to be shaped unlike anything else in creation (292), as Bunyan describes the demonic denial of every normal aspect of created nature. So, too, Christian found Apollyon to be a "monster," that is, a defiance of ordered creation, a horrible amalgam of fish, dragon, bear and lion. As De Rougemont says, "the devil is the absolute anti-model, his precise essence being disguise, the usurpation of appearances, shameless or subtle bluff—in short, the art of making forms lie."[9] When the devil appears in *Pilgrim's Progress*, it is usually in a form indicating his self-achieved fall from coherence to chaos, his denial of created being, and his compulsive enmity to all creation in its normative forms, as viewed from the perspective of the Gate.

Thus we have Christian's unavoidable struggle with Apollyon, the monster of disorder and disorientation, aberrant, abnormal, a conjunction of fragments. Apollyon manifests his nature through a conglomeration, an amassing of bear's feet, dragon's wings, fish's scales and lion's mouth (60). His essence is perversity. Yet he poses as a bearer of divine office, a rival of the Christian God, in the offices of ruler, deliverer, and forgiving judge. Accusing Christian of having deserted his earlier demonic

[9] De Rougemont, *op.cit.*, p. 14.

allegiance, he says "I am willing to pass by all, if now thou wilt yet turn again, and go back" (61). Again, "how often have I delivered" from God, he asks, "those that have faithfully served me?" (62) It is both as a perversion of creation and as a rival of God that he appears to assault Christian.

His temptation of Christian is at first an appeal to accept good from the source of evil, to take deliverance, wages and security from the demonic. When Christian refuses, Apollyon counters with a more subtle assault, grounded in truth, as he rightly accuses Christian of spiritual pride and self-righteousness: "When thou talkest of thy journey, and of what thou hast heard and seen, thou art inwardly desirous of vainglory in all that thou sayest or doest" (62). These are not idle insults, but represent the attempt to maneuver Christian in the Valley of Humiliation from his present pride to the even deeper pride of self-justification, self-defense and self-exaltation. Had Christian accepted the challenge in these terms, and sought to prove himself righteous, Apollyon would have defeated him at once and there would have been no necessity for the ensuing struggle. But Christian, despite his usual susceptibility, does not allow himself to be duped by this ruse. To Apollyon's accusation of vainglory he replies that "all this is true, and much more." Although he admits his guilt of the sin of pride, he is penitent and knows that "the prince whom I serve and honor is merciful and ready to forgive" (63). After that reply, only "grievous rage" and open assault is left for Apollyon, and the antagonists now address themselves to battle. The struggle of the

Christian against his tempter continues furiously for over half a day. Christian is several times wounded, but he later reports that just as Apollyon's victory appears certain, "I cried unto God and he heard me" (80). He is saved, in the Valley of Humiliation, by his humble recognition of the need for power beyond his own. Seizing his two-edged sword, representing both the two natures of Christ and the two testaments of Scripture, Christian drives away at his enemy until "Apollyon spread forth his dragon's wings and sped him away, that Christian saw him no more" (64).

Although Christian sees Apollyon no more, he continues to encounter the demonic, in other guises, in the waste places of the earth and in the town. Of Vanity Fair we have already spoken, but there is also the Valley of the Shadow of Death, where the demonic associates itself with the desolate, as Milton's Satan had associated himself with Chaos, for the ruin of man. "Hobgoblins, satyrs and dragons of the pit" hover over the darkness of the Valley of the Shadow of Death, where there is "a continued howling and yelling, as of a people under unutterable misery; who sat there bound in affliction and irons; and over that valley hang the discouraging clouds of confusion; death also doth always spread his wings over it. In a word, it is every whit dreadful, being utterly without order" (66). Here we have the whole sinister realm of chaos threatening creation, a fitting symbol for the life of sin which Thomas Aquinas defined as the "fall from coherence to chaos."[10]

Through this second valley Christian must also pass:

[10] Aquinas, op.cit., I-II, Q. 72, Art. 1.

[126]

"this is my way to the desired haven" (66). The Valley
of Humiliation has provided the pilgrims with the appropriate disciplines in humility which are prerequisite
for entrance into the Valley of the Shadow of Death:
man must come to terms with his own finitude of worth
before he can come to terms with his own finitude of
life. But even at best, passage through the Valley of
Death is terribly difficult. It is filled with ineffable
things, "things that cared not for Christian's sword"
(67), and that appear to Christiana under the inde-
scribable shape of evil—"a thing of a shape such as I
have not seen," she says. " 'Tis like I cannot tell what"
(254).

The demonic operation in the Valley of the Shadow
indicates the abetment of man's finiteness by the temptation to sin, just as Christian's fear of death in the Valley
of Humiliation abetted the assault of Apollyon there.
But the primary dangers of the two valleys differ: in the
Valley of Humiliation it is the assault of the self-exalting
avatar of Satan, while in the Valley of the Shadow it is
the impingement of finitude. Here man must face the
certainty of his own dissolution. Yet man as a sinful
creature seeks escape from his natural limitations, and
he rushes into sinful forms of pretense and assertion.
The basic issue, even in the Valley of Death, is, to apply
a remark from Niebuhr, "not the finiteness of man but
his sin; not his involvement in the flux of nature but
his abortive efforts to escape" from it.[11]

As Christiana's party slowly makes its way through
the Valley of the Shadow, young Joseph asks when they

[11] Niebuhr, *The Nature and Destiny of Man*, Vol. I, p. 147.

will be able to see to the end, and Mr. Great-heart replies simply: "Look to your feet" (256). So long as the
pilgrims can keep their feet on the pathway, so long,
that is, as they can faithfully accept their natural involvement in finitude and uncertainty, they are safe.
The dangers arise from man's efforts to escape that
natural involvement, to deny his own contingency under
the shadow of death. On either side of the narrow path
there is a hazard, one being a very deep and dry ditch
"into which the blind have led the blind in all ages"
(66), the ditch of a legalistically blind Pharisaism. On
the other side is a bottomless mire, the quag into which
King David fell through his lascivious desire for Bath-
sheba. Man's flight from finiteness, then, can precipitate
him either into stoic moralism or into sensual license.
"Therefore good Christian was the more put to it: for
when he sought in the dark to shun the ditch on the one
hand he was ready to tip over into the mire on the
other; also when he sought to escape the mire, without
great carefulness, he would be ready to fall into the
ditch" (67). In addition, there are pits, traps and snares,
doleful voices and hateful smells. Finally, "the mouth
of hell . . . stood also hard by the wayside" (67), and
companies of fiends patrol the valley so as to terrify and
confuse the pilgrims.

Both Christian and the company of Christians who
follow him make their way through these hazards. All
maintain their balance and all avoid the counterposed
ditches and quags by reliance upon God. The place, to
be sure, inspires anxiety, as finitude must, and this
anxiety could well overbalance them at any point along

the perilous way, but it is overcome by reliance upon God's providence. So Christian betook himself to a "weapon called All-prayer: so he cried out in my hearing, 'O, Lord, I beseech thee deliver my soul,' " and later in the face of threatening fiends he cries out "with a most vehement voice, 'I will walk in the strength of the Lord God' " (67-68), so that the fiends give way before him. With Great-heart and his company it is the same; advancing warily in prayer and in faith, they find that the fiends give way before them and their passage is completed. It is true that none of the pilgrims escapes anxiety, for although faith is determinative for them, it is not yet all-controlling. But they do have about them enough faith, a sort of minimal grace, which carries them through the way, though with fear and trembling.

Just beyond the end of the Valley of the Shadow of Death, there is a giant's cave. In the first part of Bunyan's allegory the cave is occupied by Giant Pope, and in the second by Giant Maul, a sophist. On the surface there may appear little connection between the two giants in the same cave, but allegorically there is a very meaningful connection. Both Giant Pope and Giant Sophist pretend to a knowledge beyond the limits of man's finitude, and both wish to entrap the pilgrims into similar pretense. Situated, as this cave is, on the very brink of nothingness, on the verge of the Valley of Death, its occupants pretend to an extent of knowledge and power beyond the reach of finite mind. "Man," says Reinhold Niebuhr, "is afraid to face the problem of his limited knowledge lest he fall into the abyss of meaninglessness. Thus fanaticism is always a partly conscious, partly unconscious attempt to hide the fact of ignorance and to obscure the problem of scepticism."[12] Giant Pope and Giant Maul together objectify this assertion of knowledge. The papal dignity, claiming to be infallible arbiter of religious truth, appears to Protestantism as one form of Antichrist, for as Niebuhr puts it, "a vicar of Christ on earth is bound to be, in a sense, Antichrist."[13] But in the second part of his allegory Bunyan enlarges his symbol, so that it applies to all excessive pretensions of knowledge, whether papal, protestant, or secular. The situation and the cave are the same, but the meaning is expanded. Giant Maul is the self-exalting human enemy of all humanity. Within this context, the cave itself serves as an apt antithesis to the Wicket Gate: it is an entrance which leads nowhere.

All of Bunyan's giants represent man's pretension to more than human significance. Each in his turn refuses to accept his own contingency, and all claim to be absolute masters of some portion of earth. So it is that we have the repeated disputes as to who "owns" the ground over which the pilgrims walk. Mr. Greatheart, as conductor of the pilgrims in the second part of the allegory, maintains that " 'tis the King's highway that we are in," but Giant Grim refuses to allow the pilgrims to pass over "mine own ground" (231). The giants represent an extreme human pretension which parallels the demonic pretension of the fallen angels. Their emphasis is on power, control, and domination,

[12] Niebuhr, *ibid.*, p. 185.
[13] Niebuhr, *ibid.*, p. 202.

apart from love. They seek an invulnerable autonomy. Giant Despair's self-appraisal is representative: "Now Giant Despair, because he was a giant, thought no man could overcome him" (296). None of the giants, however, are able to prevent the Christian pilgrims from pursuing the course of their journey. There are delays, battles, and even imprisonment, but the true wayfarers are never finally diverted from their ultimate goal. The very real powers, even of the power-mad, do not extend so far as to destroy the validity of the Christian's endeavor.

IV. THE VARIETIES OF APOSTASY

The pilgrims may be presented with obstacles and temptations outside themselves, but only their own actions can betray them. "Here is nothing to hurt us," Great-heart advises his charges, "unless we procure it to ourselves," and Old Honest remarks that "a Christian can never be overcome, unless he shall yield of himself" (249 and 260).

Of all the true pilgrims, Christian is perhaps the most bold, but he is also the most inclined to "yield of himself." He falls into the Slough of Despond, wanders out of the way toward the Town of Morality, sleeps on Hill Difficulty, crosses into By-Path Meadow of Giant Despair, and follows the white robed black enchanter until he is caught in a net. In no case does Christian follow an evil which he sees as an evil, but rather what appears to him to be a better way to his goal. Thus he follows the advice of Mr. Worldly-wiseman who "looked like a gentleman" (22) as he later follows the attractive black enchanter, despite a warning against the deceiving "flatterer," because he could not believe "that this fine spoken man had been he" (142). It is not at all the choice of another goal that attracts Christian from the way, for he always maintains his central dedication to the Celestial City, but he is repeatedly deluded into believing that he can find a "better" way there than the way which God has ordained for him. "At root of every temptation," as De Rougemont puts it, "lies the glimpse of the possibility of reaching divinity by a shorter road than that of reality."[14] So Christian accepts Worldly-wiseman's direction to "a better way and short," and later wanders into the grasp of Giant Despair because he "wished for a better way" (23 and 118).

Yet, with all of this erring from the way, Christian never finally apostatizes, for he always maintains his central orientation, his basic loyalty. He falls into sins and errors enough, but he holds fast to his ultimate commitment. Here we see the radical difference between the errant Christian and the apostates of the *Pilgrim's Progress*: the Christian may leave the way, but the false pilgrims repudiate the goal. Bunyan's allegory repeatedly, and in different connections, fills out the various implications of this basic distinction.

The distinction may be illustrated by several events which take place on or near the Hill Difficulty. Upon this hill, Christian finds "a pleasant arbor, made by the Lord of the Hill for the refreshing of weary travelers" and in this "ward of grace" he sits down to read from his

[14] De Rougemont, *op.cit*, p. 32.

roll "to his comfort." But he falls asleep, overtaken by an excessive comfort and self-satisfaction, and has to be aroused and urged on. Once awakened, "Christian suddenly started up, and sped him on his way, and went apace till he came to the top of the Hill" (45-6). Now at the foot of the same Hill Difficulty Bunyan had placed three other sleepers, Simple, Sloth, and Presumption, whose deep sleep cannot be broken by warnings. They see no danger in their spiritual sloth, and lack the necessary dedication to pilgrimage which could impel them along the way. The second part of the allegory shows them in another posture. As Great-heart puts it, "they were asleep when Christian went by, and now as you go by they are hanged" (225).

Christian, of course, did not escape scot free from his presumptuous sleep, for he lost his roll in the arbor and had to return for it. The allegory here is so simple that there is danger of passing it over without notice. The roll, representing Christian's "assurance of his life, and acceptance at the desired haven" (48), was lost precisely because of his over-confidence and over-indulgence. He is forced to retrace his steps in a wearisome recovery for his own misdeed, before he can continue on the road. But just before Christian turns temporarily from his goal, he encounters two men who have permanently abandoned the pilgrimage. These men, named Timorous and Mistrust, are literally running away from their salvation. "The farther we go," they tell Christian, "the more danger we meet with, therefore we turned, and are going back again" (46). "You make me afraid, but whither shall I fly to be safe?" Christian replies, and he concludes that "I must venture: to go back is nothing but death, to go forward is fear of death, and life everlasting beyond it" (46).

After Christian repudiates the apostasy of the two runners, he discovers the loss of his roll, and knows that he must return to the arbor to recover it. So he too turns his back upon the City of God, but he does so while keeping it as his habitual end. His sin, in Thomistic terms, is venial, while that of Timorous and Mistrust is mortal. "Although a man who commits a venial sin does not refer his act to God," writes Aquinas, "nevertheless he still keeps God as his habitual end. He does not decisively set himself on turning away from God, but from overfondness for a created good he falls short of God. He is like a man who loiters, without leaving the way."[15]

In other instances Christian does "leave the way," as when he betrays himself and Hopeful into capture by Giant Despair, and when they follow the "flatterer" into a net. Even then, however, Christian has not abandoned God as his chief end, but has temporarily abandoned God's appointed way as his means of advance. The real apostates, Timorous, Mistrust, and others, abandon both. Repudiating God in favor of some lesser good (safety, for example), they lose their lives by the very attempt to save them. The apostates' interest in saving their lives is a continual source of irony in Bunyan's treatment. Pliable, struggling to get out of the Slough

[15] Aquinas, *Commentary on the Sentences*, I, i, 3, in *Theological Texts*, trans. and ed. Thomas Gilby (London: Oxford University Press, 1955), p. 130.

of Despond on the side "which was next to his own house," leaves Christian to his pilgrim's hope of heaven: "May I get out again with my life, you shall possess the brave country alone for me" (16). Similarly, the two men whom Christian meets "making haste to go back" from "the borders of the Shadow of Death" urge him to turn back "if either life or peace is prized by you" (65), for they have discovered when they "were almost past coming back" that the threat of death lay before them (66). Fortunately, they say, they "saw the danger before we came to it," and so were able to save their lives (66). The superficiality of that claim underscores the central irony of self-assertion, the preserving of life now, in order to lose life eventually.

All the apostates chose their own dereliction. Despite the ultimate hazards of seeking security in a lesser city, "they will choose to go there" (227), and to abandon the larger hope of the City of God. The root of their apostasy, Christian says, is lack of "a change in their mind and will" (163), and the result is that "they love their ease more than their souls" (228). Without a proper love of God, there is no proper love for the self, and without these two loves, there can be no final persistence in pilgrimage.

7

GUIDANCE AND THE GOAL

EARLY in the first part of *Pilgrim's Progress* we discover, in Christian, a man who knows only that he must leave the City of Destruction, but who does not know where he must go or how he must make his way. Early in the second part of the allegory, Mercy, who has entered upon the way by the Wicket Gate, expresses surprise that there are still dangers and sorrows to be borne (208). Although Christian and Mercy are among the strongest and most quickwitted of the pilgrims, they are repeatedly subject to uncertainty, move slowly over the road, and, along with the others, are often confused as to what lies before them and what is next to be done or borne. Exhausted by the ardors of spiritual struggle, or confused by the perils of the way, all stand in repeated need of refreshment and of guidance. Entrance at the Gate is clearly prerequisite to arrival at the Kingdom of Heaven, yet it is equally clear that entrance alone is not enough. The pilgrims need assistance both from God and from each other if they are to attain the joys of the Celestial City.

I. CHRIST AND THE SCRIPTURES

The Scriptures are important in *Pilgrim's Progress,* although not after the fashion of that theological party which has been attacked by Karl Barth and others for

making of the Bible "a self-sufficient paper pope."[1]
Bunyan's true pilgrims do not use the Bible as a repository either of magic formulae or of inerrant proof texts.
For them, the Scriptures are primarily a guide leading
to Christ, an aid in making the pilgrimage to God.

As the allegory opens, Christian has in his hand a
book which is clearly Scripture, but, clearly too, he has
read only a part of the book, for he knows only that he
is "condemned to die" (10). This death of the soul
represents the lot of Adam, by which, as we have seen,
man condemns himself to isolation and alienation. Op-
pressed by his conviction of sin, Christian knows nothing
of hope until Evangelist comes to meet him. Evangelist
significantly gives him a new document, a parchment
roll on which is written John the Baptist's words, "Fly
from the wrath to come," a directive with a certain
muted prophetic hope. Even this is not enough, however, and Christian asks, "whither must I fly?" (11) The
reply carries with it the full implications of assurance,
as Evangelist directs Christian to the Wicket Gate, where
he will be further instructed.

This action is significant, for Evangelist does not direct
attention to what he himself personifies, that is, to the
New Testament writings, but rather directs Christian
to the person of Christ as the Gate to everlasting life,
and as the "shining light" by which he can find his way
(11). "The object of faith," according to Kierkegaard,
"is not the teaching but the teacher,"[2] and so it is here.
John Baillie defines precisely the view of revelation im-

[1] *Barth's Dogmatics*, p. 61.
[2] Beach and Niebuhr, *op.cit.*, p. 427.

plied here: "Instead of saying that 'Scripture as a whole is the Whole with which Revelation is to be identified,' we shall prefer to say of Scripture, as itself says of John the Baptist, 'He was not that light, but was to bear witness to that light.' "[3] So it is that Evangelist, citing John the Baptist, points not to himself but to Christ as the way, the truth, and the light. By no other means, Christian later declares, could he have found the Gate (51).

Thus early in the allegory, Holy Scripture has shown Christian both his need for, and the way of, redemption. It does more, for it indicates the meaning of redemption: everlasting life in divine community, "loving and holy . . . in the sight of God; and standing in his presence with acceptance forever" (15). Again, all is centered upon God and man's relation to him.

Throughout, there is a deepening of understanding on Christian's part, a vitally progressive revelation. This progression is indicated in part, at least, by the successive manuscripts which Christian studies. At the outset there is the book, clearly the book of the law, in terms of which Christian learns his own failure, the failure of Adam. Then comes the further revelation of Evangelist, who gives Christian the John the Baptist roll and directs him to the Gate. Later, at the cross, Christian acquires an even more personal understanding as another roll is given to him, representing the ultimate application to himself of what he knows. The Scriptures now become fully and existentially relevant to him as "the

[3] John Baillie, *The Idea of Revelation in Recent Thought* (New York: Columbia University Press, 1956), p. 125.

assurance of his life and acceptance at the desired haven" (48). The roll of assurance comes to him after his burden of guilt has fallen into the empty sepulchre, when he is ready for the restoration of relationship; as he takes the roll, he accepts the fact of his own acceptance by God.

In this incident we have underscored again the relationship of Scripture as written words to Christ as the living Word. Christian understands the relevance of Scripture to himself in terms of the crucifixion and resurrection. What happens to Christian at the cross, as he loses his burden and finds his ultimate acceptance, comes as something "very surprising to him" (40). He had already "believed," in the sense of giving his intellectual assent to what he knew of God, but here, knowledge and assent give place to faith to free Christian of his weighty burden. He has already known and accepted the Scriptural accounts of God's plan of salvation, has been instructed in it at the Gate and at the Interpreter's House, but he has not yet become involved in it in the fulness of his personality. At the cross his faith becomes saving, that is, it becomes applicable in the reformation sense of a complete reliance on the mercy and love of God.

This event can take place only in consequence of Good Friday and Easter, when God's mercy and justice, his love and power, join in restoring man to his true humanity. Christian has long been trying, without success, to achieve this, and it comes to him only when he is in the presence of the cross and sepulchre, standing figuratively between the atonement and the resurrection, between the symbols of God's act of blotting out sin and God's act of restoring life. It is within the new context of this event that Christian finds the Scriptures to be the gospel of his salvation, a source both of strength and of refreshment for him as he follows the course of his pilgrimage.

Throughout that pilgrimage the figure of Christ is determinative. It is through Christ as the Gate that Christian enters the way, and it is the sight of Christ at the end which inspirits Christian as he passes through the river of death to enter the Celestial City. Christianity is defined, not merely by doctrine, but through a person, with the clear implication that it must be expressed in terms of a life. "The Truth," as Kierkegaard puts it, "in the sense in which Christ was the Truth, is not a sum of sentences, not a definition of concepts, etc., but a life."[4]

These primary distinctions are ignored by certain of the pseudo-pilgrims, who treat the Scriptures only as a repository of proof texts or as a sourcebook for doctrine. The first error is exemplified in Mr. Self-will, who though "he never came in at the Gate that stands at the head of the way," nonetheless "pretended himself to be a pilgrim" and found "warrant" in Scripture for whatever he wilfully wished to do (268-69). Although he is a vigorous citer of Biblical passages, Self-will's references are always taken apart from the total context and apart from the normative person of Christ.

Whereas Mr. Self-will never seems to arrive at a total system of doctrine, his concern being the immediate justification of particular whims, Mr. Talkative has so

---

[4] Beach and Niebuhr, *op.cit.*, p. 431.

thoroughly mastered Biblical theology that he is, in his expressions, a near-perfect model of orthodoxy. He will talk upon any subject: "of things heavenly, or things earthly; things moral, or things evangelical; things sacred, or things profane; things past, or things to come; things foreign, or things at home; things more essential, or things circumstantial: provided that all be done to our profit" (82). He has reduced theology to a highly skilled intellectual game, succumbing to the danger of what Kierkegaard called becoming "erudite instead of becoming a Christian."[5] His opinions are, in general, eminently sound, but he has left them unrelated to existence, justifying himself by his knowledge without regard to his life. For this reason Christian says of him that " 'tis better to deal with a Turk than with him" (84). He has obtained "great knowledge . . . in the mysteries of the gospel," as Faithful observes, and yet without grace of soul, for "a man may know like an angel, and yet be no Christian" (87-88).

The truth to be found in Scripture is not "a sum of sentences," but a way of life leading to God, and the knowledge to be sought in it is, as Hopeful finds, a knowledge of "the beauty of Jesus Christ" which "made me love a holy life" (153). Repeated study of Scripture as the vehicle which carries knowledge of the divine action through Christ, and insistent prayers for understanding, eventually bring Hopeful to the time when "the Father showed me his Son" (151). Christian de-

[5] Soren Kierkegaard, *Concluding Unscientific Postscript to the Philosophical Fragments*, trans. David Swenson and Walter Lowrie (Princeton: Princeton University Press, 1941), p. 540.

scribes this experience as "a revelation of Christ to your soul indeed" (152), and it is significant that it comes neither in materialistic form nor in visionary ecstasy. "I did not see him," Hopeful comments, "with my bodily eyes, but with the eyes of my understanding" (151). As Christian had recognized at the cross, so Hopeful now understands, *comprehends*, the full relevance of Christ for his own existence. "What is believing?" he asks, and then replies that "believing and coming was all one." So, with "my heart full of joy, mine eyes full of tears, and mine affections running over with love," he set out on the pilgrimage to God (152). Late in the second part of the allegory, Mr. Valiant-for-truth telescopes, with customary incisiveness, the entire process: "It was so. I believed and therefore came out, got into the way, fought all that set themselves against me, and by believing am come to this place" (309).

Scripture is basically concerned to show man his own need—Christian's "What must I do to be saved?"—and God's offer of salvation. These complementary effects are perfectly symbolized by the "looking glass" for which Mercy develops such an attachment, a mirror which, as an emblem of the Scriptures, "would present a man, one way, with his own features exactly, and turn it but another way, and it would show one the very face and similitude of the Prince of Pilgrims himself" (301-2). In Scripture are combined the recognition of alienation and the means of restoration.

Scripture is also useful in other ways to the pilgrims. It is the sword with which the Christian warriors defend themselves from attack by demonic agents seeking their destruction, as in Christian's battle with Apollyon and Valiant-for-truth's victorious use of the "right Jerusalem blade" against his assailants (305). So employed, the sword is an apt emblem for the settled assurances of God, used to beat down the malevolent pretensions of Satan, and to protect the ·individual whose value is properly assessed in terms of divine love rather than of demonic hatred. Another important symbol treats Scripture as a map or chart of the way for the guidance of pilgrims. It is in this allegorical sense that Mr. Great-heart, by consulting his "book or map" (312), saves his company from falling into a trap set for them in the Enchanted Ground. Later, Great-heart "struck a light," and Scripture becomes a source of illumination by which the pilgrims may see to pass through darkness over an unknown way (313). Though new to the pilgrims, the way is actually a very ancient thing: "it was cast up by the patriarchs, prophets, Christ, and his apostles" (29). It is, in fact, the very way described throughout Scripture, so that for its passage the Scriptures are the best available chart and light.

Perhaps the most inclusive single symbol for Scripture comes in one of the later sets of verses which Bunyan inserts into his narrative. Great-heart is describing the company which he is conducting, and the goal of their pilgrimage:

First here's Christiana and her train,
Her sons, and her sons' wives, who like the wain
Keep by the pole, and do by compass steer
From sin to grace, else they had not been here.
  (298)

A poor enough attempt at poetry, these lines are admirably succinct and direct allegory. The pole is, of course, Christ, to which the compass of Scripture points, and it is by this compass and this pole that the pilgrims plot their course "from sin to grace."

II. THE HOLY SPIRIT AND THE CHURCH

Being a book about God, the Bible can only be fully understood under the guidance of God, for the purpose of Scripture is not to impart inert factual information but to lead to a vital relationship with deity. God is indeed to be "found" through the Scriptures, but not in the letters themselves, nor in the printing of the text. The Apostle Paul makes the point succinctly: "the letter killeth, but the spirit giveth life,"[6] and again, "we should serve in newness of spirit, and not in the oldness of the letter."[7] It is through the spirit of God, the Holy Spirit of the trinitarian economy, that the Scriptures become meaningful and relevant for men. The Scriptures are therefore to be understood in reliance upon God's guidance, in the divine *persona* of the Holy Spirit.

But Scripture, by means of which individuals may be led to God, is not merely an individual's book. It is also a community book, the importance of community being stressed both in the Old Testament and in the New. In the first, the decisive community is Israel, or the faithful remnant which represents the true Israel, whereas in the second, the decisive community is the Church, the New Israel. Scripture and Church are inseparably

[6] II Corinthians 3:6.   [7] Romans 7:6.

united, and within the trinitarian economy God manifests himself in both, through the operations of the Holy
Spirit. Without the Spirit, a person may read the words
of Scripture and yet not encounter the Word of God;
and without the Spirit as the true vicar of Christ, an
ecclesiastical organization may exist, but not be a true
Church. Apart from the Holy Spirit's guidance, then,
neither the reading of Scripture nor the work of the
ecclesia is effective to its purpose.

In Bunyan's Interpreter we find the clearest suggestion of the Holy Spirit. The Interpreter is a complex
figure, not to be understood only as a symbol for the
Holy Spirit. It is more accurate to say that he suggests,
rather than represents, the Holy Spirit. But suggest he
surely does, and in very significant ways. At the Gate
Christian is told (30) that the Interpreter will "show
him excellent things," just as Christ promises his disciples that the Holy Spirit will "teach you all things."[8]
The Interpreter's House stands next in the way after
the Gate, as the Holy Spirit proceeds after Christ to
continue the divine operation in history. In his own
terms, the Interpreter shows "that which will be profitable" to pilgrims, and his first act after admitting Christian to his house is to light the symbolic candle called
"Illumination" (30-31). In our earlier treatment of
Paradise Lost we dealt at length with the doctrine of
accommodation, whereby the divine reality condescends
to human categories of expression. Here, in the illumination which the Holy Spirit supplies, the believer is
enlightened so that his mind may move from the human

[8] John 14:26.

expression to the divine reality. Calvin defines this operation when he writes that the "Holy Spirit by his illumination makes us capable of understanding those things which would otherwise far exceed our grasp."[9]

After he has lighted the candle, the Interpreter shows Christian the picture of a very dignified person, whose eyes are fixed on heaven, who has the "Law of Truth" upon his lips, the world behind his back, a crown of gold over his head and who, with the Scriptures in his hand, "pleads with men" (31). This man bears the traditional symbols of the true Reformed pastor, the true minister of God, and as such is "the only man whom the Lord of the place whither thou art going hath authorized to be thy guide in all difficult places" (31). Others, Christian is advised, may "pretend to lead thee right, but their way goes down to death" (31). The function of this pastor is clearly ministerial, rather than magisterial. He brings children to birth, that is, he brings men to Christian regeneration, and nurses them through their religious childhood. "His work is to know and unfold dark [i.e., obscure] things to sinners" (31), and to lead them to the Celestial City. In all of these ways he acts as an instrument of the Holy Spirit, implementing God's concern for men.

The true Reformed pastor, here represented in a portrait hung upon a study wall, is given living personification in the second part of *Pilgrim's Progress* when the Interpreter sends Mr. Great-heart to conduct Christiana and her company. What was passively symbolized by the painting is now actively exhibited by Great-heart, who

[9] *Theological Treatises*, p. 105.

guides, instructs, nourishes, and guards his charges through all the dangers and trials of pilgrimage. What was done by the Interpreter—who "knows all things" (260)—in each of these areas, is carried on by Greatheart as his deputy.

The landscape of pilgrimage, then, is trinitarian. The way itself is the Father's, "the King's highway," and the Gate is the Son, through whom alone entrance may be found into God's way, while the Holy Spirit is suggested by the Interpreter.

The Interpreter's House is the earliest of Bunyan's great symbols for the Church, although in the first part of the allegory only the Church's teaching function is fully developed under the symbol of the House, while the communal and sacramental aspects are at best only suggested. Christian is taught, among other things, the meaning of grace, the work of Christ, and the value of patience, and then is sent on his way. The Interpreter pronounces a parting benediction, which gives promise that "the Comforter," another name for the Holy Spirit, will accompany and strengthen him on his way (40).

With Christiana and her party the Interpreter's House becomes a far broader symbol for the Church. There is a communal rejoicing of all those within at her appearance, as "they all smiled for joy that Christiana was become a pilgrim" (211). There is still the "illumination" of the Holy Spirit, and still instruction, but now there is a much clearer sense of community than before, when Christian's only society was with the Interpreter himself.

The change is appropriate, for, as we have already observed, Bunyan has provided a three-dimensional view of the Christian life by the stereoscopic device of picturing two separate pilgrimages over the same way. The Christian life is primarily represented in its distinctively individual aspects in part one, and in its distinctively corporate aspects in part two. Although the two parts are mainly developed in this way, they are not exclusively devoted to individual and communal meaning, for there is much of individual significance in the experiences of Christiana's party, while in Christian's pilgrimage many kinds of symbols represent the Church. There is, for example, the companionship with Faithful and Hopeful, of which much has already been said, and there are also the Christian communities which lie along the way—House Beautiful, the Delectable Mountains, and Beulah Land—of which more will be said shortly.

For the present, however, it would be well to indicate certain features that distinguish the true Church from all those outside it who also appear in *Pilgrim's Progress*, and to notice some of the primary distinctions between the Church and the world. It is obviously not enough to say that the Church is made up of those who follow the road of pilgrimage, for there are as many false pilgrims as true. Nor is it enough to say that the Church is distinguished by a desire to reach the Celestial City, for again there are those who seek heaven only for its joys, apart from the love of God. Formalist and Hypocrisy are two such, who "come tumbling over the wall" to join Christian a bit before the Hill Difficulty. Not only do they not come in at the Gate, but they stay only briefly on the way, soon choosing the easier paths marked Danger and Destruction. But they declare that their goal is the Celestial City, and that they "are going for praise to Mount Sion" (42). The phrasing is a fine example of ironic effect, with the double-entendre of "going for praise," apparently indicating the praise of God, but actually disclosing the inner motivation of false wayfarers who make the pilgrimage in order to be praised themselves. They seek heaven as a source of rewards, not as a state of communion with God. Furthermore, as is always true in *Pilgrim's Progress*, their names are highly significant, particularly as Hypocrisy is joined with Formalist to indicate the type of formalism being condemned. Bunyan is pointing to a use which makes religious forms into what Calvin called "lurking places where [men] safely played with God," imagining that when "they thrust external pomps upon him, they have by this artifice evaded the necessity of giving themselves."[10] In defense of their practices, however, Formalist and Hypocrisy proudly declare that "what they did they had custom for, and could produce, if need were, testimony that would witness it for more than a thousand years" (42). Despite the antiquity which they claim for their tradition, they clearly do not represent the Church.

Neither do Mr. By-ends and his companions, who come upon Christian and Hopeful beyond Vanity Fair, "go over" to Demas' silver mine, and are never "seen again in the way" (115). By-ends is a particularly interesting character. Like Old Honest, he refuses to disclose his name, but for reasons of worldly prudence, far re-

[10] *Ibid.*, p. 193.

moved from the humility of the true pilgrim. He is,
indeed, totally innocent of humility, and talks as if he
"knew something more than all the world doth" (106).
Although he cannot yet appeal to a thousand years'
tradition—"my great grandfather," he admits, "was but
a water-man, looking one way and rowing another, and
I got most of my estate by the same occupation" (105)—
he nonetheless finds himself well-connected in the present establishment within his native country of Fair-
speech. Great lords, ladies and ecclesiastics of his town
are related to him, and all seems well. " 'Tis true," he
confesses, "we somewhat differ in religion from those of
the stricter sort, yet but in two small points: First, we
never strive against wind and tide. Second, we are always
most zealous when Religion goes in his silver slippers;
we love much to walk with him in the street, if the sun
shines, and the people applaud it" (106). All in all, he
promises the pilgrims, "you shall find me a fair com-
pany-keeper, if you will still admit me your associate"
(107).

Christian and Hopeful are quite willing to admit
By-ends, provided only that he will, when necessary,
"go against wind and tide" and retain steadfast loyalty
to "Religion in his rags, as well as when in his silver
slippers, and stand by him too, when bound in irons, as
well as when he walketh the streets with applause"
(107). This stipulation is too strict for By-ends, who declares with characteristic self-assurance that "I shall
never desert my old principles, since they are harmless
and profitable" (107).

Bunyan obviously relished drawing the portrait of

By-ends, perhaps because he had seen many examples of this religious type in the course of his life. As always, he is eminently fair in his treatment, and gives By-ends his own say. After Christian and Hopeful forsake him, By-ends is joined by three old friends and schoolfellows, Mr. Hold-the-world, Mr. Money-love, and Mr. Save-all, and to them he gives his own highly colored account of why he is walking alone. "The men before us," he explains, "are so rigid and love so much their own notions, and do so lightly esteem the opinions of others, that let a man be never so godly" (By-ends is, ironically, "never so godly"), "yet if he jumps not with them in all things, they thrust him quite out of their company." Demonstrating his charge of intolerance, By-ends adds that "they are for holding *their notions*, though all men are against them, but I am for religion in what, and so far as, the times and my safety will bear it" (108).

The others heartily agree with By-ends, as by pious phrases and Biblical citations taken out of context they buttress their own position. Together they are perfect examples of what Kierkegaard called "a worldliness which would have the name of being Christian, but would have it at a price as cheap as possible."[11] But they are not of the true Church, despite their pretensions.

The Church, then, is to be defined neither by mere profession nor by an apparent commitment to the goal and the way. Obviously, too, the Church is not to be recognized by the personal perfection of its members, for were it to be constituted only of the "perfect" there would be no members, and Christian, surely, could

[11] Beach and Niebuhr, *op.cit.*, p. 433.

never qualify. On this point Luther wrote that "we do not preach the doctrine that the Spirit's office is one of complete accomplishment, but rather that it is progressive; the Spirit operates continuously and increasingly."[12]

Although the Christian remains imperfect, his basic loyalties are established, and they commit him to the Kingdom of God rather than to any of the lesser loyalties which make up the Kingdom of this world. The Church's loyalty is to God, and the churchman's citizenship is in the Celestial City, however far removed he may be from it. Thus, in Vanity Fair, there *must* be a difference between the conduct of the pilgrims and that of the inhabitants. The citizens of Vanity Fair are its natives, and although both Christian and Faithful are themselves native to the city of Destruction, they have, in New Testament terms, been "reborn" as citizens of heaven, so that their primary allegiance is radically realigned, and they have become "strangers and pilgrims in the earth" in contradistinction to those who are "strangers to pilgrimage" (291). In that distinction we see a primary difference between the Church and the world. When Christian chooses, above the enticements of Apollyon, the service, wages, servants, government, company, and country of Christ, he is merely declaring his particular patriotism, the true mark of the Church. Pilgrimage, then, is an inescapable act of the Christian, who makes his way to the center of his commitment in the country of God.

Against this background we can understand the place of the sacraments in the pilgrim's life. At root, the

[12] Luther, *A Compend of Luther's Theology*, p. 71.

Latin word *sacramentum* meant an oath, particularly a military oath of allegiance to the standard. The Latin word was used to translate the New Testament Greek *mysterion*, or mystery, indicating the virtue which, though not at once apparent, lay behind the outward symbol. It is the outward sign which is extended by the minister, whereas the thing signified is extended by the Holy Spirit. And the sacraments, like the Church to which they exclusively belong, are closely related to the Scriptures. But both are founded on faith, with faith understood as "a firm and solid confidence," as Calvin defines it in terms general to the entire Reformation, "by means of which we rest surely in the mercy of God which is promised to us through the gospel."[13] For the relation of sacrament and Scripture, Calvin gives this apt explanation: "Let us abide by this conclusion, that the office of the sacraments is precisely the same as that of the Word of God, which is to offer and present Christ to us, and in him the treasures of his heavenly grace; but they confer no advantage or profit without being received by faith, just as wine, or oil, or any other liquor, though it be poured plentifully on a vessel, yet it will overflow and be lost, unless the mouth of the vessel be open; and the vessel itself, though wet on the outside, will remain empty and dry within."[14]

Appropriately, the sacraments are first encountered in *Pilgrim's Progress* at the Interpreter's House, because the symbols of the sacraments are presented by pastors

[13] John Calvin, *Instruction in Faith*, trans. and ed., Paul T. Fuhrmann (Philadelphia: Westminster Press, 1949), p. 38.
[14] Calvin, *Institutes*, trans. Allen, IV, xiv, 17.

whom the Holy Spirit has commissioned, while the graces symbolized are themselves presented only by the Holy Spirit. In the first part of the allegory, reference is made only to the sacrament of baptism—when water is sprinkled over the dust of sin so that it may be effectively swept away (32)—but in the second part we have a full treatment of both sacraments, in their proper order. First there is "the bath Sanctification," in which the pilgrims are all washed to "make them clean from the soil which they have gathered by travelling" (219). Having submitted to baptism in willingness and faith, as the outward sign of the removal of the guilt of sin, they emerge "not only sweet and clean, but also much enlivened and strengthened" (219). For Bunyan, baptism can be either a sprinkling or a bath, and he opposed making obstacles to faith out of differences of opinion on this point. After baptism comes holy communion, the new Passover of the new Israel, with which faith is sealed, just as "the children of Israel did eat when they came out from the land of Egypt." Having been administered this second and sealing sacrament, the pilgrims find that their faces are now "more like them of angels" (219-20), since they have partaken of the sustenance of heaven. But, significantly, they cannot see the same glory in themselves which they see in each other, and the result is therefore a Christian humility by which "they began to esteem each other better than themselves" (220).

Beyond the Interpreter's House, the Church on pilgrimage finds the next great symbol of churchly nurture in House Beautiful. Here, Christiana and her companions are served the sacramental meal of "a lamb, with the accustomed sauce belonging thereto." When they have partaken, and "ended their prayer with a Psalm," they retire for rest to a room called "Christ's bosom" (234). This progression of symbols is particularly revealing, for the pilgrims have eaten, in their earthly journey, of elements signifying the completed sacrifice of the historical Christ; the Lord's Supper prepares them for rest in a chamber which, by its very name, signifies the heavenly beatitude awaiting them at the end of their journey, as well as the sustaining support along the way. The earthly communion, taken in faith, is indivisibly related to the celebrations of the Celestial City.

A later administration of communion at House Beautiful further indicates its uses. Earlier in the pilgrimage, Christiana's son, Matthew, ate fruit from the devil's orchard (241). The fruit, as sin, cannot be digested by the human system, and Matthew falls into a critical illness. "He must be purged," says Dr. Skill, the physician, "or else he will die" (241). Several medicines are tried, all representing laws and ceremonies by which men try to relieve themselves of their sins, but with no success. A stronger medicine must be prescribed, and so Dr. Skill prepares and administers a purgative especially designed to restore the sick to health, a purge made from the body and blood of Christ: "*Ex carne et sanguine Christi*," Bunyan writes, and adds with charming honesty, "the Latin I borrow" (242). To these elements he adds the appropriate promises, recalling the divine promises of redemption associated with the sacrifice of Christ, and "a proportional quantity of salt," representing the grace of God by which human savor is preserved. But, in addition to the work of God and of the administering physician of souls, something also is required of Matthew, if the purging of sin is to be effective. The medicine must be taken with prayer and fasting, and with "the tears of repentance" (242). When all was done, and "after a short prayer for the blessing of God upon it," Matthew took it, "and it wrought kindly with him . . . and did quite rid him" of his disease (242).

The use of communion here is clearly medicinal and therapeutic, for the relief of sickness abnormally induced among men by the perversion of Satan. Sin is posited as a disease, a dislocation of the human norm intended by God, and is cured only by the conjunction of divine initiative and human response. The already accomplished sacrifice of Christ, and the long-given promises, are not in any sense re-enacted, but are presently applied to the living person. There must also be the grace of God, along with human effort and repentance. With faithful prayer, these ingredients complete the transformation of the original "elements" offered to Matthew by Dr. Skill. The result is saving, that is, salve-ing, for "salvation" is the restoration of human wholeness and health. "These pills are good to prevent diseases, as well as to cure," Dr. Skill says, and "if a man will but use this physic as he should it will make him live forever" (243). The sacramental symbolism is complete.

Other instances of the sacrament occur in *Pilgrim's Progress*, as when young James becomes sick with fear in the Valley of the Shadow (254), and there are a large number of communal meals. Some of these may be interpreted as sacramental, but they generally provide more than bread and wine, and seem to signify the more ordinary, non-sacramental intercourse of the Christian community. As such, they are quite significant. Perhaps they recall the *agape*, or love feasts, mentioned in the New Testament, but whether or not this is one of their references, they do serve as apt emblems for the life of the Church as one of shared experience and communal worship.

In eating the food set before them in the various houses and resting places along the way, the pilgrims are eating the bread by which they live; but they do not live by bread alone, and these meals signify more than the satisfaction of appetite, although that in itself is important enough. They indicate the communal support and sharing of the community, the mutuality of the Christian life, expressed in the most common acts of human existence. Further, these common acts are filled with a new and transcendent significance, as the table set in Gaius' house begets "a greater desire to sit at the supper of the great King in his Kingdom," for all that happens in the Christian's experience of real earthly joy is "but as the laying of the trenchers, and as setting of salt upon the board, when compared with the feast that our Lord will make for us when we come to his house" (275). The food itself is significant: the milk represents the milk of Christian nurture, butter and honey symbolize God's Word, the hard-shelled nuts signify difficult or obscure texts, and apples are eaten as a sign of the basic goodness of all God's material creation, which retains its purposed goodness despite the misuse of "apples" by Adam and Eve (276).

In the Lord's Supper, then, we see the Church in communion with God, while in the common meals we see it in community with itself under God. Bunyan makes clear in the *Pilgrim's Progress* that there is a third dimension of community in the life of the Church— the communion of saints by which the present Church is linked with the Church of all ages. In addition to their other functions, the houses along the way preserve the traditions of the past and make them vivid and vital for later wayfarers. In the Interpreter's House, the instruction almost entirely concerns meaning and action, and in the House Beautiful, there is still doctrinal catechising, but there is the added element of instruction in the great tradition. The damsels read to Christian of "the worthy acts" of God's servants, and histories of many "things both ancient and modern" (57). They also show him "rarities" which have been assembled for the edification of pilgrims, a collection which includes Moses' rod, the jawbone of the ass with which Samson fought the Philistines, and the stone used by David in slaying Goliath (58). Christiana is also shown through the collections, and sees such wonders as the forbidden fruit, Jacob's ladder, the anchor of hope, and even the altar and the knife with which Abraham was prepared to sacrifice Isaac (245-46). Clearly these "relics" are actual, but actual in an intellectual, rather than physical sense. Clearly, too, they are used only for instruction, and not for the honor accorded to the relics of the Roman Church; but just as certainly, Bunyan has inserted them in his allegory to demonstrate the important place of tradition in the Reformed Church.

At Gaius' house the pilgrims are further instructed in the history of the Church. As the focus in House Beautiful is divided between the Old and the New Testament Church, to indicate the continuity of the Church as the "Israel" of God, this continuity is extended through and beyond the times of Scripture, as Gaius recounts the faithfulness of Stephen, James, Paul, and Peter in the first century, together with the later martyrdoms of Ignatius, Romanus, Polycarp, and others, bringing the account of faithfulness into the present by reference to "four such boys as these," Christiana's sons (273-74). Finally, at the very end of the pilgrim's way in the land of Beulah, there is "a record kept of the names of them that had been pilgrims of old, and a history of all the famous acts that they had done (318).

Bunyan variously indicates the proper respect in which the great "saints" are to be held. Everywhere, of course, Christiana encounters the honor still being paid to Christian, and her sons fully evidence the true reverence for holy men in their attitude towards their father: "The boys take all after their father, and covet to tread in his steps. Yea, if they do but see any place where the old pilgrim hath lain, or any print of his foot, it ministreth joy to their hearts, and they covet to lie or tread in the same" (273). The only proper dulia or reverence for "saints" is imitation in the patterning of one's own life. Similarly, there is no petitioning to them, although there is prayer about them, prayer of

thanksgiving to God for their lives and historical influence. So it is that the later pilgrims stop when they come
to the place of Faithful's martyrdom, and thank God
who "had enabled him to bear his cross so well, and
the rather, because they now found that they had a
benefit by such a manly suffering as his was" (293).

It is now apparent that Bunyan's pilgrims regard
themselves as a part of the communion of saints in all
ages and all places. They are but the present, visible,
and earthly contingent of an invisible Church which
extends beyond them into the past and into the future,
and which will be totally assembled in the kingdom of
heaven at the end of the world's history.

III. THE END OF THE PILGRIMAGE

Both for the visible Church as a whole and for the
individual, the pilgrimage to heaven is filled with
dangers until the very end. The Enchanted Ground lies
just before Beulah Land, and is "one of the last refuges
that the enemy to pilgrims has" (313). Filled with pits
and blanketed in darkness, it is so tiresome a way as to
tempt pilgrims to stop before completing their journey.
It is here that Madam Bubble attempts to restrain Stand-
fast, saying that "I am the mistress of the world, and men
are made happy by me" (315). It appears that one of
the later stratagems of the demonic is to impede the
pilgrim, weary him past endurance, and so arrest his
progress short of the goal; another is to tempt by exalted
pretensions of a lesser good, calling on the pilgrim to
abandon his ultimate fulfillment.

Two other major types of temptation come to divert Christian and Hopeful in the latter stages of their journey, and between the four demonic assaults the strategy of hell is summarized. As Christian and Hopeful move from the Delectable Mountains towards the Enchanted Ground they are approached by a man who is significantly described as "black of flesh, but covered with a very light robe" (141). Just ahead is a branching of the way into two paths, both of which "seemed straight." Here, instead of consulting their map, they consult with the stranger, a fine spoken man who claims he is going to the Celestial City and is willing to lead them there. But the path on which he takes them "by degrees turned" so that in a "little time their faces were turned away from the City," and they find themselves caught in a net. "With that, the white robe fell off the black man's back; then they saw where they were. Wherefore there they lay crying some time, for they could not get themselves out" (141). Again, however, their human penitence is met by the divine initiative, and "a shining one" (142) releases them from the net.

Their second temptation is of quite a different order, as they encounter Atheist, who has openly turned his back on the way and is retracting his steps. The Celestial City, he tells them, is a mere delusion, without reality of any kind, and if they persist in the way they will have nothing but their travel to reward their pains. The pilgrims repudiate this temptation, and Atheist, "laughing at them, went his way," to return to his own city and to enjoy the good things which would be available to him there (144-45).

The later temptations are now fully delineated, and may be summarized in this manner: the way itself is so difficult that pilgrims are inclined to rest and fall asleep, so that "none can wake them" (313). There is also the overt appeal of Madam Bubble that the travellers should settle for a lesser good, abandoning the quest for the greatest good. Again, there is the white-robed devil who, in the guise of an angel of light, promises to lead men to the Celestial City and leads them instead into a net. Finally, there is Atheist, who denies the very existence of the City itself, and seeks to convince pilgrims that their struggles are without reason and goal.

In no case is appeal made to evil as such, although, in each instance, yielding might have lead eventually to the absolute and unrelieved evil of hell. As De Rougemont puts it, "it is not evil in itself which tempts, but always a good which one imagines an even better good than that which God offers, or else which one imagines to be more suited to oneself."[15] It is within this context that the demonic, representing the presumptuous exaltation of a lesser good, "solicits" man to pursue his own destruction under the guise of following a fuller life. The interaction between an outward proffering of the lesser good and an inward consent to it constitutes apostasy.

Among the most notable apostates of *Pilgrim's Progress* is Turn-away, who figures in both parts of the

[15] De Rougemont, *op.cit.*, p. 33. See also Richard Hooker, *Of the Laws of Ecclesiastical Polity*, i, vii, 4-7, in *The Works*, ed. John Keble (New York: D. Appleton & Company, 1849), Vol. i, pp. 166-67.

allegory. The pilgrimage is almost completed when Christian and Hopeful first see him, bound and being led away by a company of devils who thrust him down the byway to hell (133). Here the demonic aspect is pictured as decisive. But the demonic action is powerless to achieve human damnation without the willing co-operation of man. Man must embrace his own damnation, and so in the second part of *Pilgrim's Progress* the treatment of Turn-away differs markedly from that of part one. Mr. Great-heart describes his end, not in terms of seven demons thrusting him bound into hell, but rather, in terms of his willful resistance to Evangelist and escape over the wall, out of the pilgrim's way. What Great-heart describes as Turn-away's "escape" over the wall, Christian and Hopeful see as his damnation by the powers of darkness. Here we have another example of Bunyan's stereoscopic technique, where disparate visions of a single incident or of a single landscape are beautifully fused into a single texture of meaning: the devils do indeed thrust Turn-away into hell, but they do so because of Turn-away's choice of separation from God. Turn-away is "bound" to go to hell, must go to hell, as the state of final separation from God, because he has willfully repudiated the divine acceptance offered to him by Evangelist. Under these conditions, heaven becomes an impossibility, and hell the only reality.

Heaven is also an impossibility for Atheist. Not knowing God, he must deny heaven, just as modern secular man, divorced from closeness with God, inevitably repudiates the life everlasting of Christian vision. We admire Atheist for his honesty far more than we do those false pilgrims who sentimentally persist in pursuing heaven for the sake of its "comforts," without the desire for God.

As for the Christian pilgrims, they value heaven not for its benefits but for God, and find heaven because they love God. They see all things increasingly in the light of God, and they learn to value all men, including themselves, according to the love of God. They refuse the evaluations of Apollyon, or the giants, or Madam Bubble, or Vanity Fair, or of any of the other seducers. The basic temptation in each instance is to accept a different pattern of evaluation from that of God. Thus when Pragmatic, Inconsiderate, and Wild-head demand that Valiant-for-truth repudiate his search for life eternal, he replies that "my life cost more dear far, than that I should lightly give it away" (304). The Gate remains the norm, and the final evaluation of human existence is established by the "cost" of Calvary. As the Almighty places such an infinite value upon individual lives, the Christian pilgrims know that they will be everlastingly preserved as individuals in the divine love. Within this vision of truth, "he that forgets his Savior is unmerciful to himself" (215), whereas, conversely, seeing "the beauty of Jesus Christ" leads Hopeful to "love a holy life" (153), and Mercy "to fall in love with her own salvation" (197). The pilgrims, recognizing themselves as sinners, value their lives because God values them, and set out for heaven in order to see, serve, love, and enjoy the God of their salvation (238).

The enjoyment which will be full in heaven is present, in part, even on the difficult way of pilgrimage, as the wayfarers sing that "we, tho pilgrims, joyful lives may live" (303). The extent of present joy possible to the pilgrims depends upon individual temperament, so that some like Mr. Fearing can play nothing but sad music, while the lives of others are filled with joyful songs (266-67). But even for the most doleful, a faithful vision of the cross will make the heart "more merry and blithe" and with those like Christiana who are of a more sanguine disposition the heart is "ten times more light-some and joyous" than it was before (224). At each of the churchly houses along the way there is music, song, and rejoicing, as the Christians "did eat and drink, and were merry" (283). At House Beautiful, Mercy aptly summarizes: "Music in the house, music in the heart, and music also in heaven, for joy that we are here" (234), as the joys of heaven and earth flow over and into each other.

In each sphere, the Christian's joy is the product of his faithful relationship to God. In heaven, this relationship is direct and maximal, whereas on earth, it is variously impeded so that man, whether saved or unsaved, in greater or lesser degree repudiates his chief end in the service, love, and enjoyment of God. Some of the pilgrims cross the River of Death in an exalted state of communion with God, while others cross with sinful and self-centered fears, as does Christian who, despite all that he knows and all that he has experienced, exalts himself even in the River by judging himself more severely than God judges him. His very concentration upon his sins, and his moralistic weighing of them, constitutes a defection from God, a sinful dependence on his own judgment rather than on the divine judgment. "Forgiveness," Reinhold Niebuhr writes, "is as necessary at the end as at the beginning of the Christian life,"[16] and Christian irrevocably accepts the fact that forgiveness has been granted only when his thoughts are diverted from himself to Christ. From that time on, his passage of the River is peaceful, for his life is oriented upon its true center. His sinful separation from God is buried in the River of Death.

The vision of life in the Celestial City is complex and elaborate. It must be so, for the life everlasting is not a simple reabsorption of souls into the divine, as in the higher Eastern religions, but is a continuity of persons, as individuals, in the presence of God; it joins the individual's consummation with that of society in the heavenly communion of saints. Man, as truly man, cannot fully exist apart from God and from other men, so that heavenly fulfillment unites the two great commandments, now everlastingly satisfied—the love of God and the love of neighbor. There is the dual context of living in the presence of the divine, and surrounded by the company of the faithful of all ages. Here is the only truly human society, without alienation and divisiveness, united in the wholeness of the ultimate praise of God, welcoming each newcomer as an increment to the communal joy: "But glorious it was, to see how the open region was filled with horses and chariots with trumpeters and pipers, with singers and players on stringed instruments, to welcome the pilgrims as they went up

[16] *The Nature and Destiny of Man*, Vol. ii, p. 105.

and followed one another in at the beautiful gate of the City" (326).

The self-exalting debasement of Adam, the archetypal Everyman, is now left behind, as the fully individual Christian is everlastingly established in the loving community of heaven. The drama of history is completed. "There were also of them some that had wings, and they answered one another without intermission, saying, *Holy, Holy, Holy is the Lord.* And after that, they shut up the gates; which when I had seen, I wished myself among them" (172).

8

EPILOGUE

Our dialectical exchange between theology on the one hand and *Paradise Lost* and *Pilgrim's Progress* on the other has now been concluded. Through this dialectic we have examined certain major symbols, themes, and doctrines, as they appear in the Christian faith in general and these two works in particular. Our purpose was not to compare the epic and allegory with each other, but to bring each in turn into dialogue with the Christian tradition to which they belong, with the intent of making both the individual works and the encompassing tradition more meaningful.

As we saw in the first chapter, poetry appeared to Milton and Bunyan to be a particularly useful vehicle for conveying the themes of Christian thought and life, because literary method is closely akin to the literary forms of Scripture in symbol, metaphor, parable, and story. It was through such forms that Milton and Bunyan treated Christian truth in *Paradise Lost* and *Pilgrim's Progress*. Both men were concerned with transmitting, through literary creation, the essentials of Christian faith and life. They were, furthermore, in general agreement as to those essentials, and each displayed a large measure of tolerance toward variations in doctrinal detail. In sum, each was concerned both with saving faith, as a new and vital relationship to God, and with the new life which develops from that faith.

These and many other convictions Milton and Bunyan shared. The cast of their minds, however, differed
markedly. Milton was the superbly educated, intellectual sophisticate, Bunyan the shrewd, self-taught tinker.
Personally unacquainted with each other, and writing
without coordinated purposes beyond those which came
from belonging to the broad tradition of seventeenth-
century Puritanism, they produced two works which
were not only literary masterpieces, but which supple-
mented each other so remarkably that between them
the entire compass of Christian thought and life is
developed with singular completeness.

Paradise Lost was a panoramic view of creation and
providence, nature and history, a sweeping survey of
all existence as it appeared to the greatly learned mind
of a Christian humanist. Bunyan, on the other hand,
chose a focus more restricted, more intimate and immediately pragmatic, concerning himself with the common experiences of men. Milton, as a Christian intellectual, focused primarily on the Christian understanding
of life, while Bunyan, an itinerant mechanic and
preacher, was largely concerned with the Christian conduct of life. Both concerns are necessary, and each work,
as we have clearly and repeatedly seen, represents both
to some extent; but the distinction between their major
emphases remains helpful in understanding these two
works in terms of the Christian faith, and the Christian
faith through these two works.

To recapitulate all that we have observed thus far
would be both tedious and gratuitous. To summarize
the theological conceptions with which both men dealt

would require us, unnecessarily, either to recite (with modifications) some classical creed, or to write a new creed, which is not the purpose of this book. We may, however, recall briefly some of the chief points at which *Paradise Lost* and *Pilgrim's Progress* supplement each other, each serving to continue, reinforce, or complete the emphases of the other. The major figures of both works are God, man, and Satan. Let us look first at Satan.

The actions of Bunyan's pilgrims when confronted by the demonic agents along the way are patently based on traditional Christian conceptions of evil. Bunyan repeatedly refers, either explicitly or by inferential symbols, to those conceptions, but he never develops them at great length. Milton, on the other hand, provides an extensive analysis of evil, an analysis which for depth, breadth, and general perceptiveness, is unequalled in Christian literature. While Bunyan is primarily concerned with individuals reacting to the threat of evil, Milton seeks to develop a total view of the evil by which mankind is beset. His is an entire landscape of sin, a full history of the origin and course of demonic life. He provides a biography of Satan, along with a family, a court, political alliances, and strategies of assault upon men. The demonic is a graphic type of life, a way in which the self relates to itself and to other selves. Bunyan displays less interest in the demonic as such. The background and nature of Apollyon are assumed, rather than discussed in detail, as Christian gets directly to the business of defeating him. Where Milton "solves" the problem of the demonic, so that mankind may meet and overcome its influences, Bunyan assumes a prior and sufficient understanding of the demonic, and has Christian fight it. That Bunyan's demonic agents are generally sub-angelic, whereas Milton's are generally angels, underscores the distinction between a major concern with pragmatic events, and the essential problem underlying such events.

As with the demonic, so it is with the human. Milton analyzes man as such, the archetypal man Adam, rather than individual men or types. His concern is with the nature of mankind, with human betrayal of human nature, and with the results of that betrayal, moving from the general to the specific. Adam's experience of temptation and his commission of sin is universally applicable—man's attempt to make himself divine. Although Bunyan accepts this view of the originating and universal sin, he concentrates, in *Pilgrim's Progress*, on how sin operates in different individuals. Thus Christian's besetting sin is vanity and vainglory, Faithful's is fleshliness, and so on. Bunyan's many characters respond variously to the common experience of pilgrimage. His focus is the characters as individuals and as types, whereas Milton's emphasis is on Man and Woman. Even from the mount of vision in *Paradise Lost*, Milton's men are not displayed so individualistically as are Bunyan's, but remain purveyors of larger Christian understandings and more general Christian insights into institutions, social forces, and historical developments.

The same distinction holds with the divine. Milton is concerned with developing poetically as full an understanding of God as is possible by means of accommodation, so that man may know the ground of his own being. Man cannot understand himself apart from a knowledge of God, but knowing God and God's will for mankind, man can see himself both as he is and as he should be. By an epic vision of God planning creation and redemption from all eternity, Milton roots man's life in the providence of God, rather than in chance or circumstance. Man's life is divorced from meaningless-ness and futility, and endowed with value, dignity, and purpose. Milton poetically mirrors in his epic the revela-tion of God as found in the Christian Scriptures and as analyzed by Christian thought. Bunyan, on the other hand, takes all this for granted, and, without ever bring-ing God directly on stage, he teaches about God through the acts, experiences, and aspirations of men.

In these and other ways, Milton and Bunyan supple-ment each other, and delineate the full compass of Christian thought and life, Christian understanding and conduct. To approach *Paradise Lost* and *Pilgrim's Prog-ress* together in this fashion is not only to understand the Christian tradition better, but also to see each of these works more clearly. Neither work restricts itself only to thought or to life, as both areas are within the province of each. It could not be otherwise, for as Bun-yan puts it, "believing and coming was all one" (152). By considering the full range of the works placed side by side, we are more amply prepared for appreciating the fulness of each in its own right; by considering the two in connection with theology, we find that literature and theology alike are benefited. Both for the Christian and for the non-Christian, profound insights and great beauties are available in *Paradise Lost* and *Pilgrim's Progress*, and it is to the epic and allegory themselves that we should now turn, with what I hope will be a larger awareness. Criticism is never an end in itself, but has for its end the purposes of literature. Bunyan, thus, may be allowed the last, appropriate word:

> yet let Truth be free
> To make her sallies upon thee and me,
> Which way it pleases God: For who knows how,
> Better than he that taught us first to plow,
> To guide our mind and pens for his design?
> And he makes base things usher in divine. (6)

BIBLIOGRAPHY OF MAJOR WORKS CITED

Aquinas, Thomas. *Introduction to Saint Thomas Aquinas,* ed. Anton C. Pegis, New York: Modern Library, 1948.

——. *Nature and Grace, Selections from The Summa Theologica of Thomas Aquinas,* trans. and ed. A. M. Fairweather (as *The Library of Christian Classics.* Vol. xi), Philadelphia: Westminster Press, 1954.

——. *Theological Texts,* trans. and ed. Thomas Gilby, London: Oxford University Press, 1955.

Augustine. *Basic Writings of Saint Augustine,* 2 vols., ed. Whitney J. Oates, New York: Random House, 1948.

——. *Earlier Writings,* trans. and ed. J. H. S. Burleigh (as *The Library of Christian Classics,* Vol. vi), Philadelphia: Westminster Press, 1953.

Baillie, Donald M. *God Was In Christ: An Essay on Incarnation and Atonement,* New York: Charles Scribner's Sons, 1948.

Baillie, John. *And The Life Everlasting,* New York: Charles Scribner's Sons, 1948.

——. *The Idea of Revelation in Recent Thought,* New York: Columbia University Press, 1956.

Bainton, Roland H. *Here I Stand, A Life of Martin Luther,* New York: Abingdon Press, 1950.

Barth, Karl. *Dogmatics in Outline,* trans. G. T. Thomson, New York: Philosophical Library, n.d. (c. 1947).

Beach, Waldo and Niebuhr, H. Richard, eds. *Christian Ethics, Sources of the Living Tradition,* New York: The Ronald Press Company, 1955.

Bible. *The Interpreter's Bible,* 12 vols., ed. Nolan B. Harmon, New York: Abingdon-Cokesbury, 1952-57.

Boethius. *The Consolation of Philosophy,* ed. H. F. Stewart, New York: G. P. Putnam's Sons, 1918.

Bruner, Emil. *Dogmatics,* 2 vols., trans. Olive Wyon, London: Lutterworth Press, 1955.

Bunyan, John. *The Pilgrim's Progress,* ed. James Blanton Wharey, Oxford: Clarendon Press, 1928.

Calvin, John. *The Institutes of the Christian Religion,* 2 vols., trans. John Allen, Philadelphia: Presbyterian Board of Publication, n.d.

[175]

Calvin, John. *The Institutes of Christian Religion*, trans. Thomas Norton, London: John Norton, 1611.

————. *Instruction in Faith*, trans. Paul T. Fuhrmann, Philadelphia: Westminster Press, 1949.

————. *Theological Treatises*, trans. J. K. S. Reid (as *The Library of Christian Classics*, Vol. xxii), Philadelphia: Westminster Press, 1954.

Cranmer, Thomas. *The Works of Thomas Cranmer, Archbishop of Canterbury, Martyr, 1556*, 2 vols., ed. John E. Cox, Cambridge: Cambridge University Press, 1844.

De Jesus-Marie, Pere Bruno, ed. *Satan*, New York: Sheed and Ward, 1952.

De Rougemont, Denis. *The Devil's Share*, trans. Haakon Chevalier, New York: The Bollingen Foundation, 1952.

De Sales, Francis. *The Spiritual Conferences*, trans. Abbot Gasquet and Canon Mackey, Westminster, Maryland: The Newman Bookshop, 1943.

Dowey, Edward A., Jr. *The Knowledge of God in Calvin's Theology*, New York: Columbia University Press, 1952.

Harbison, E. Harris. *The Christian Scholar in the Age of Reformation*, New York: Charles Scribner's Sons, 1956.

Hardy, Edward R. and Richardson, Cyril C., eds. *Christology of the Later Fathers* (as *The Library of Christian Classics*, Vol. iii), Philadelphia: Westminster Press, 1954.

Hendry, George S. *The Holy Spirit in Christian Theology*, Philadelphia: Westminster Press, 1946.

Heppe, Heinrich. *Reformed Dogmatics*, ed. Ernst Bizer, London: George Allen and Unwin, 1950.

Hooker, Richard. *The Works*, 2 vols., ed. John Keble, New York: D. Appleton & Company, 1849.

Kierkegaard, Soren. *Attack Upon Christendom*, trans. Walter Lowrie, Princeton: Princeton University Press, 1944.

————. *Concluding Unscientific Postscript to the Philosophical Fragments*, trans. David Swenson and Walter Lowrie, Princeton: Princeton University Press, 1941.

————. *A Kierkegaard Anthology*, ed. Robert Bretall, Princeton: Princeton University Press, 1951.

Knox, John. *On the Meaning of Christ*, New York: Charles Scribner's Sons, 1947.

Luther, Martin. *A Compend of Luther's Theology*, ed.

Hugh Thomson Kerr, Jr., Philadelphia: Westminster Press, 1943.

McNeill, John T. *The History and Character of Calvinism,* New York: Oxford University Press, 1954.

Milton, John. *De Doctrina Christiana,* trans. Charles R. Sumner (in *The Works of John Milton,* ed. Frank A. Patterson et al., Vol. xiv), New York: Columbia University Press, 1931-38.

————. *Paradise Lost,* ed. Merritt Y. Hughes, New York: Odyssey Press, 1935.

Niebuhr, Reinhold. *Discerning the Signs of the Times, Sermons for Today and Tomorrow,* New York: Charles Scribner's Sons, 1946.

————. *The Nature and Destiny of Man, A Christian Interpretation,* 2 vols. in 1, New York: Charles Scribner's Sons, 1949.

Outler, Albert C. *Psychotherapy and The Christian Message,* New York: Harper and Brothers, 1954.

Pascal, Blaise. *Pensées and the Provincial Letters,* trans. W. F. Trotter and Thomas McCrie, New York: Modern Library, 1941.

Quistorp, Heinrich. *Calvin's Doctrine of the Last Things,* trans. Harold Knight, Richmond: John Knox Press, 1955.

Schweitzer, Albert. *An Anthology,* ed. Charles R. Joy, Boston: Beacon Press, 1947.

————. *Christianity and the Religions of the World,* trans. Johanna Powers, London: George Allen and Unwin, 1951.

————. *Out of My Life and Thought,* trans. C. T. Campion, New York: New American Library of World Literature, 1953.

Temple, William. *William Temple's Teaching,* ed. A. E. Baker, Philadelphia: Westminster Press, 1951.

Tillich, Paul. *Systematic Theology,* Vol. i, Chicago: University of Chicago Press, 1953.

Weber, Otto. *Karl Barth's Church Dogmatics: An Introductory Report on Volumes I:1 to III:4,* trans. Arthur C. Cochrane, Philadelphia: Westminster Press, 1953.

Whitehead, Albert North. *Religion in the Making,* Cambridge: Cambridge University Press, 1927.

INDEX OF SUBJECTS AND AUTHORITIES

INDEX

Cocceius, Johannes: on fall, 60; on freedom, 75

communion, sacrament of: 154-57

communion of saints: 158-60

community: destroyed by demonic, 40-41; man requires, 45-47; God restores, 84; in heaven, 88, 166-67; in church, 144, 147, 157-58. *See also* heaven, and love

conformity: 120, 122

conscience: 60, 83, 114

consummation: 166-67

contingency: 130

contrition: 67, 69

convenient, the: 99-100, 106

convention: 108

Cranmer, Thomas: on faith, 72-73

creation: demonic antipathy to, 22, 28, 37, 38, 124; good, 30; and accommodation, 62. *See also* demonic, and perversion

death: and sin, 36-38, 55, 57, 77; soul's, 59-60, 89, 137; desire for, 61, 66; dominance of, 64; fear of, 75; God's purpose for, 86-87; meeting, 127-28, 165-66

deception: human, 57. *See also* demonic, and fraud

degeneration: human, 56, 80-81. *See also* demonic

demonic: characteristics and functions, 22-25, 68, 100-01, 127, 142-43; seeks power, 23, 26; repudiates love, 23, 26, 29, 32; abandons freedom, 23, 35; degeneration, 23-24, 30, 36, 38-39; deceptions, 23, 28, 117, 122, 124, 162; disguises and poses, 26, 36, 121, 124-25; possession by, 29-30, 33, 36; destruction, 29, 30, 36, 59, 64, 66, 97, 98, 101, 123, 162; compared with man, 42, 130; strategies, 120-22, 160-62; evaluation of man, 143. *See also* Antichrist, perversion, and self-deification

De Rougemont, Denis: on demonic anti-model, 22; on demonic disguises, 121-22, 124; on temptation, 132, 162

De Sales, Francis: on presence of God, 119

dialectic: 168

didacticism: 6

discord: 48

divine: *see* God

dualism: 21

dulia: 159

Easter: 139

ego-ideal: 35

escape: 72, 73, 80, 96, 127-28

eternal, the: 100

eternal life: 87-91

Everyman: *see* man

evil: meaning of, 21, 30; its ultimate destruction, 78, 86-88; active and passive resistance to, 123-24. *See also* demonic, and sin

faith: defined, 72-73, 81, 153; and works, 73; and knowledge, 75, 139; a final relationship, 83; growth of, 84, 129; its object, 137

fall of man: 45, 48, 51-55, 60, 89; compared with fall of rebellious angels, 42, 67-68, 78, 130; results of, 56, 62-66, 80-81. *See also* fortunate fall, man, self-deification, and sin

fanaticism: 129-30

fear: sinful, 55, 60-61, 75, 102-03; types of, 101-04, 133-34; pious, 102

feeling of God's presence: 119

figurative, the: 15, 26. *See also* accommodation

finitude: 127. *See also* death

forgiveness: 166. *See also* reconciliation

formalism: 149, 155

fortunate fall: 74, 80, 85

fraud: 68. *See also* deception

freedom: and the demonic, 23, 25, 27, 35-38; meaning of, 34, 35, 48, 75-77, 82; and man, 42-43, 51, 70, 76-77, 80, 83, 163. *See also* slavery

frustration: 34

fulfillment: 26, 54, 98
fundamentalism: 8, 136-37

Genesis: 15, 62
genocide: 66
God: anthropomorphic accommodations, 9-14; symmetry of love and power, 26, 76; respect for man, 42-43, 51, 76-77, 83, 164; created man for community, 62; his grace, 70-71; his anger, 71, 77; his providence, 74, 78, 86, 91. *See also* Christ, Holy Spirit, Son of God, and trinity
Good Friday: 139
grace: prevenient, 67, 84; meaning of, 70-71; growth in, 74-75, 81, 84, 85, 98, 110, 113, 129, 152; and freedom, 82
guilt: 70, 95. *See also* sin

happiness: 44-45. *See also* joy
harmony: 29, 44, 48
hatred: demonic, 22, 29, 32; of self, 32-33, 61, 101; of God, 61; God's, 77-78
heaven: compared with hell, 32, 40, 44, 89, 116-17, 163; sought apart from God, 44, 148; nature of, 47, 88, 98-99, 101, 109-10, 164, 165-67
hell: nature of, 24, 33, 38-41, 87; compared with heaven, 32, 40, 44, 89, 116-17, 163; fear of, 102-03
Hendry, George: on freedom and grace, 82
Holy Spirit: general operation of, 82-83, 152; in the church, 83, 144-47, 152; illumination of Scripture, 144-46; in sacraments, 152-54. *See also* revelation
Horace: 74
humanism, Christian: 8
humanity: 104-05
humility: 126, 150, 154

idolatry: 54, 56, 58, 122. *See also* self-deification
ignorance: 118-19

illumination: 144-46. *See also* Holy Spirit
image of demonic: 64
image of God: 44-45, 62, 64. *See also* man
immorality: 72
immortality: 87-88. *See also* life everlasting
impasse: 80
incarnation: *see* Christ, and Son of God
Indian religion: 21, 87, 90
infallibility: 130
information: 144. *See also* tree of knowledge
instruction: 147, 154-55, 158
integrity: 42, 51, 55-56
intolerance: 151
involvement: 127-28
irony: 27, 30, 50, 57, 135, 149, 151
isolation: *see* alienation

joy: 32, 81, 84, 157, 164-67. *See also* happiness
judge, divine: *see* Son of God
judgment: *see* man, and Son of God
justice: 78

Kierkegaard, Soren: on the convenient and the eternal, 99-100; on love and fear, 102; on object of faith, 137; on Christ as Truth, 140; on pretenses to religion, 141, 151
kingdom of evil: 121
kingdom of God: *see* heaven
knowledge: and faith, 3, 75, 139, 141; of the demonic, 27; and wisdom, 50; of God and the self, 96, 142; pretentious, 129-30. *See also* tree of knowledge
Knox, John: on transfiguration, 11

labor: 43-44
language barrier: 65
legalism: 83, 111, 115, 128, 155. *See also* moralism, self-righteousness, virtue, and works
license: 128